Major General Willia...Earle

MAJOR GENERAL WILLIAM EARLE Major General Earle, Liverpool's only ever General, was born in Hope Street in 1833, educated in a Liverpool private school, following which he went to Harrow. He joined the Army in 1851, serving in the 49th. Regiment where he was conspicuously brave in battles of the Crimean War including those at Inkerman and Sebastopol, for which he received honours from England, Sardinia and Turkey.

From the post of Lieutenant in 1855 he worked his way up to Major General in 1880. Service in Egypt eventually found him, in 1882, in command of the garrison at Alexandria, from where he set off in 1884 as part of the force to relieve General Gordon. Part way up the Nile, the force was split, one column going to the aid of General Gordon, Earle's troops being sent to punish the tribes who had murdered previous parties of our men in the area.

On Feb.10th. 1885, Earle was in command of a small party of men in the Sudanese hills near Berti and, at Kirbekan, they encountered the enemy, some of whom were concealed in a stone hut. Earle, in a display of typical brave abandon, and despite the shouts of warning from his officers, rushed the hut, only to be shot in the head from which injury he died. He was brought back home and is buried in Allerton. The statue to Liverpool's great hero is by C.B.Birch and was unveiled by Lord Wolseley on Dec 16th. 1887.

Fig.4- Major-General Earle

The Cenotaph

Although the function of a cenotaph is to remind us of all things grim and sad, a few minutes spent studying the carving of this memorial can be most rewarding.

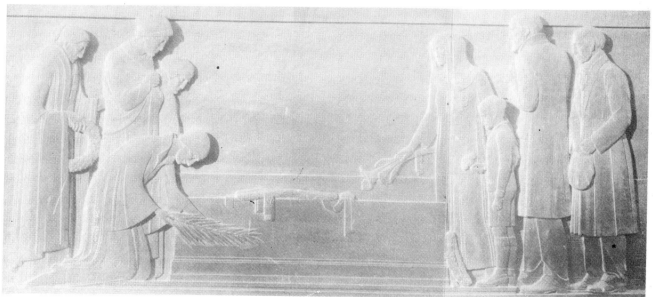

Fig.5- Side of Cenotaph, the Mourners

It was was designed by Professor Lionel Budden of Liverpool University and the sculpture is by local man, H.Tyson Smith, whose work is to be found on buildings and monuments all over the City.

By the time that a site had been decided upon for a memorial, the Great War was long finished and this does, in fact, rank as quite a late symbol of remembrance for those lost in the squalor and misery of the trenches. As mentioned previously, the statue of Disraeli was moved to clear the site for the Cenotaph for which there was an open competition to find a suitable design.

Fig.6- H.Tyson Smith

Amazingly, there were no fewer than 767 designs and 39 models entered from points all over the world yet, despite submitting his entry only 48 hours before the deadline, local man Tyson Smith won the prize. He and Professor Budden had collaborated on their design and there was unashamed rejoicing in the fact that the competition had been won by local men in the face of such oppposition! Even so, some of the professionals were so insanely jealous that the wooden mock-up that was erected on site had to be placed there at 7.30 a.m. and removed very soon afterwards because there had been strong rumours that Tyson Smith's rivals were determined to wreck it! More will be written about the sculptor in a companion book to be published soon but, suffice it to say that, by this time, Tyson Smith was well known for his work and had already established himself as a specialist at designing war memorials (Birkenhead, Southport, Accrington &c.)

Fig.8- Side of Cenotaph, Soldiers

One of Tyson Smith's team of seventeen sculptors, a Mr. James Mc.Laughlin, still pursues his art in the same studios in the rear of the Blueccoat Chambers, still heated by the stove given to Tyson Smith by artist Augustus John! Mr.Mc.Laughlin helped to create the Cenotaph and was able to identify some of the characters depicted thereon. On the left side, the lady standing behind the kneeling mourner is Mrs. Tyson Smith. On the right, the boy standing is her son and the man himself is to be seen further to the right with his hand in his jacket.

Fig.7- The Cenotaph

The Twenties style of dress worn by the mourners is interesting and deserves detailed study by the observer. As a contrast, the reverse side depicts the relentless march of the grim faced soldiers, so many of whom were lost forever in that most terrible of wars.

It is a strange phenomenon that birds are never seen to rest on war memorials and it is rare to see them defaced by their droppings. Could this be because the creatures instinctively associate these constructions with death?

The rather un-English sounding word, Cenotaph, is, in fact, derived from Greek words meaning tomb and indicating that it is a monument to the deceased while not actually containing any remains of the persons as would a mausoleum. The word was rarely heard until 1920 when Sir. Edwin Lutyens designed the Cenotaph in London's Whitehall.

This monument was unveiled by Lord Derby on 11th. November 1930.

The Wellington Column

Opposite the Art Gallery stands this 132ft. high column of Darleydale stone, the foundation stone of which was laid by the Mayor, S.R.Graves Esq., on 1st.May 1861. It was designed by George Anderson Lawton of Glasgow and is said to be an exact replica of Edinburgh's Melville monument.

It was 5 o'clock in the afternoon on May 16th 1863 that the then Mayor, Mr.R.C.Gardner, accompanied by the High Sheriff, Sir.William Brown,Bart., travelled from the Town Hall in the State Carriage followed by various dignitaries and members of the Wellington Memorial Committee. They were greeted by a vast throng gathered by the column, including 2200 pensioners and volunteers who were commanded by Col. Sir John Jones K.C.B.. The Committee spokesman, Mr.John Torr, formally presented the memorial to the Mayor and City, whose acceptance was marked by the firing of a salvo of 19 guns by the volunteers.

Fig.9- Wellington atop his column

Wellington was still held as quite a hero at that time, 11 years after his death and the monument is worthy of him. The carved panel near the base of the column shows the Grand Charge at the Battle of Waterloo and the 14ft. figure of Wellington, by G.A.Lawson, is said to have been cast from melted-down guns salvaged from the battle-field. In the panel, the Duke can be seen on his horse, telescope in hand, and he appears to be holding the telescope in the main figure as well.

He was born, Arthur Wellesley, in Dublin in 1769 and was educated in Chelsea, Eton and Brussels, being described at school as "aloof and aggressive". His widowed mother sent him to military academy in France for a year and yet, six years later, in 1763, he had worked his way up to become Lt.Colonel of the 33rd.Foot Regiment, now known as the Duke of Wellington's Regiment. By 1796, after various military experiences, he found himself in India having by then firmly decided on making his career as a soldier. His eventful spell in India was punctuated by a period of illness which, by preventing his taking a passage on a troopship to Egypt, saved his life as the aforesaid vessel sank with no survivors.

Having learnt everything about military and civil life in India, he then tired of that country and returned home in Sept. 1805. His busy life included more miltary campaigns, re-election to Parliament and marriage in 1806. Following a victory against the French in 1809, he was made Viscount Wellington, the name being taken from that of the village near his home village of Wellesley from which was derived the family name. In the Peninsular War he forced the French out of Portugal and Spain, receiving many more honours from grateful friends in the process. To most people, it is his part in the defeat of Napoleon at Waterloo that gave him lasting fame, but his exploits took him to many other places whose names are now unknown to most of us, although they are listed at the base of the column.

By 1818 he was back in politics, attaining the post of Prime Minister for two stormy years, 1828-30. He was never universally popular, and at one time even had to have steel shutters fitted to the windows of his home for protection from the mob! His career is quite involved and those wishing to research it in more depth should visit Apsley House, Wellington's London home, to see the astounding display of gifts, trophies and honours heaped upon him by by grateful rulers and governments of countries whom he helped in their struggles against their foes.

A local connection with Wellington is in 1850 when he came for the opening celebrations of the Liverpool to Manchester Railway.

Wellington died on 14th. Sept.1852 and his funeral, which was described as one of the great spectacles of the century, was as impressive as had been his career. A magnificent funeral carriage, made from the melted-down guns of Waterloo, was drawn by twelve black horses past 1½ million people to St.Paul's Cathedral where, after a four-hour gas-lit service, attended by 20,000 people, his body was lowered into the crypt where it lies to this day.

Fig.10- The panel depicting the Battle of Waterloo

Steble Fountain

The fountain was the gift of Lt.Colonel Richard Fell Steble, born in 1835 at Lindal Mount near Ulverston. He trained in law and practiced in that profession from 1852 to 1870, when he retired having become the owner of a large property. Presumably his well-earned financial independence then gave him the urge to enter public service.

In 1859 he had become interested in matters military, firstly becoming a volunteer, by 1870 having attained the rank of Lt.Colonel of the First Lancashire Rifle Volunteers. He was Mayor of Liverpool from 1874-5, living in Sandfield Park, West Derby.

The fountain was designed by W.Cunliffe and erected in 1879, being formally handed over to the Corporation on May 1st. of that year. It was made by Allen & Co. of Lambeth Hill, Upper Thames Street near St.Paul's Cathedral, but only office blocks stand on the site of the foundry today. Although the official inauguration took place on May 1st., there were those who said that it would have been more appropriate if it had been on April 1st. instead as the monument suffered teething troubles which were siezed upon with great delight by "The Porcupine", a satirical weekly paper of the time! The wind sweeping up the hill was blamed for the "lop-sided squirt of dirty water which issues from the top of the fountain". It was said that far finer effects were produced by a "barman washing the windows of a grogshop by the use of a hose!" Blaming the height-to-base width ratio for the spillage of water at full pressure, it was suggested that cab-drivers' shelters be placed alongside, minus the roof, and that a "penny shower" be set up for the benefit of the citizens! By June 7th. of that year it was said that the fountain "played in a most villianous manner!"

Fig.11- Neptune and ladies

Fig.12- Fine details of the Fountain

Two modern sources give the four figures around the base of the fountain as representing the four seasons, but contemporary sources suggest otherwise and it is those that appear to be correct. The figures are Neptune, Amphitrite, Acis and Galatea. The God of the seas, known as Neptune in Roman mythology and as Poseidon in the Greek tales, was also the creator of the first horse. Also in the watery depths lived many other spirits, many of them descendants of Oceanus, an ancient Titan god. One of Oceanus's daughters, Doris, married a likeable old man-of-the-sea called Nereus and between them they produced fifty beautiful daughters known as Nereids, who had the appearance of mermaids and spent their carefree days frolicking in the surf and generally having a good time. Their home was in a cave quite near to Neptune's palace and one of them, Amphitrite, caught his eye, and eventually marrying him at a tremendous ceremony held on the ocean floor!

Neptune had a trident with which he stirred up the sea and also a silver horn which he would blow in order to summon all of the water-spirits to his palace. It was to his son, Triton, that he gave the horn as a special gift.

Fig.13- Fountain detail

The year before, when the gift of the fountain was received from Mr.Steble "with acclamations of delight", the proviso was that it should not be at any cost to the ratepayers. What had been (possibly conveniently) forgotten was that £400 was required for a steam-driven pump to operate the water flow. Incredible as it sounds to us now, it was actually stated that there was no shortage of money in Liverpool, but the Corporation complained at having been deceived. The steam engine was located in the basement of St.Georges Hall and, on August 23rd., the Porcupine reported that there was heard in the Crown Court "a mysterious throbbing, apparently proceeding from the very foundations of the Earth". "The dreadful subterranean throb....drove them to the verge of madness!" The reporters "were about to close their notebooks and rush from the Court and cast themselves into the sea!" The Judge was apparently about to "sieze his matchless wig, with the intention of tearing it to fragments, stamping upon the pieces and hanging himself with the strings!"

But, just in time, a messenger arrived, having discovered the source of annoyance, the steam engine, the engineer being ordered forthwith to quench his fire, stop the engine and release the steam down the drain, following which, peace reigned supreme once more in the upper floors! We still have our subterranean rumbles what with Merseyrail running beneath many buildings, but nowadays nothing gets done, we just have to suffer!

Another of the Nereids was called Galatea, one of her admirers being the Cyclops Polyphemus, an ugly one-eyed giant who stood no chance because Galatea had fallen madly in love with a handsome Sicilian shepherd-boy called Acis. She probably met Acis when she was romping in the surf on the beach. As is often the case, jealousy rears its ugly head, and one day, when Acis and Galatea were alone together and happy in each others' company, Polyphemus surprised them, killing poor Acis with a big rock. According to legend, Galatea wept so much and for so long that she was transformed into a fountain and Acis, her dead lover, was, transformed into a river, occurences that appear to be considered quite normal in those days! To this day the River Acis still flows in Sicily near Mount Etna although it is not recorded where Galatea's fountain can be found.

Looking nearby, notice the old Standard Measures plaque showing feet and yards, quite a rarity nowadays and the only one in the city as far as I know.

Fig.14- Standard Measures plaque

The Folly Fair

The Steble fountain and Wellington's column stand on a triangular plot of land once known as the Folly Fair. Long ago there stood a windmill on this spot, which was taken down in 1780, the site being subsequently levelled and paved. It was on this land that the Folly Fair was held on Easter Monday and Tuesday each year. The strange name originated from a tea-house and strawberry garden owned by a Mr. Gibson, the manager of the Theatre Royal. This delightful-sounding place was situated on what is now Islington, at the junction with Christian Street. Onto the tea-house Gibson built an enormous and totally incongruous eight-storey look-out tower, soon acquiring the name of Gibson's Folly! The road became Folly Lane in which was held the Folly Fair.

A popular pastime in those days was "lifting" whereby the men sought to lift the women on Easter Monday and vice versa on the following day! This ancient custom was said to be symbolic of the resurrection. Mr.Picton, writing in 1875, tells us that "it was impossible for a female to pass through any of the lower streets of Liverpool on Easter Monday without being laid hold of by a set of good natured ruffians who asked for "baksheesh" which, if not granted, ended up with her being heaved three times in the air!" The following day was almost as lively for the men!

Gibson's Folly was pulled down in 1780 to make way for a grand house for a Mr.Phillip Christian.

As is often the case, what starts as innocent fun ends up going too far and the Folly Fair became a "saturnalia of drunkenness, debauchery and fighting". Attempts by the small police force to prohibit the fair failed until, in 1818, the space was railed off and filled with small shops, then to be called Islington Market. The Folly Fair moved to where Stafford Street is now, but it died out within a couple of years.

St.John's Gardens

The area now known as St.John's Gardens has a history dating back at least as far as 1743 when it was recorded that the Council ordered "to plant hedges on the Great Heath and grass for the inhabitants to dry clothes", the Great Heath being what we know now as St.John's Gardens. In 1767 the area was consecrated for use as a graveyard; on June 24th. 1775, the first stone being laid for the new St.John's Church which was eventually consecrated in 1784. Prior to the creation of the gardens as we see them today, the church was acquired by the Corporation, the last services held on March 27th. 1898, the church being demolished soon afterwards.

At one time, the area had been earmarked as a possible site for the new proposed cathedral, to be built to replace St.Peter's in Church Street. Sir.William Emerson won a competition for a design in 1887 but nothing ever became of it and they decided to make a garden on the site instead. The gardens cost £24,000 to create and were opened on June 29th. 1904 by the Chairman of the Parks & Gardens Committee, Alderman Joseph Ball J.P.. Soon nicknamed "the stoneyard" for its large collection of statues, it nevertheless contains some fine works by the leading sculptors of the day, there being some very interesting stories behind the figures represented here. The stone walls around and within the gardens are in the classic Edwardian tapering style, but the loss of the railings in the last war rather detracts from their intended design.

In 1935, following the opening of the new Mersey Tunnel, there featured an article in the January edition of "The Liverpolitan" detailing the proposed plans for a monstrous bus station on the site of the gardens to service the planned bus routes through the tunnel. They were going to "scoop away St.John's Gardens" as "no longer can the bustling and congested City afford the luxury of a large garden here"! Thankfully, this plan was never implemented, and it is ironic that the proposed Liverpool-Wirral bus service had to wait until the opening of the Wallasey Tunnel in 1971! The only tenuous link with the former ecclesiastical use of this site is the presence of 230 French seamen buried here having died in jail as prisoners of war during the Napoleonic Wars. A plaque to these men was erected opposite the Gladstone Memorial on Armistice Day 1924, the day chosen to symbolise the fact that England and France had just fought as allies in the Great War.

We shall now look at the statues, in no particular order of importance, to see what we can find out about these great men.

Alexander Balfour

Born on 2nd. Sept. 1824 at Levenbank, Fife, Alexander Balfour was the son of a foundry owner. Educated at St.Andrew's, he worked for his grandfather until 1844 when the onset of a financial depression drove him to Liverpool in search of work. With a couple of friends, in 1851, he set up the firm of S.Williamson & Co., to trade with Valparaiso in Chile. The partners went abroad drumming up business, while Alexander stayed in Liverpool handling affairs at this end of their operations. In common with the practice of the day, they owned shares in ships rather than buying them outright, and they did quite well. Alexander married Jessie Roxburgh in 1864, and eventually made the trip to Valparaiso where he started a school for English-speaking people, also helping the Church there and becoming one of the founders of the YMCA.

Fig.15- Alexander Balfour

The business later expanded into California but, although they were operating in areas where there was not too much opposition, their trading route was via the notorious Cape Horn with all its treacherous weather and currents. Life on board the sailing ships was grim at the best of times, but at Cape Horn it was particularly bad. In order to keep out the sea, the forecastle area, where the men lived, had to be sealed up, rendering it unbearably stuffy. No fires were allowed in case of accident and, to make it even worse, fresh food had usually run out by the time the ship reached this part of the journey. The men would have to spend hours clinging to the yard-arms, wet through no matter what clothes they

wore and with no way of drying out for days on end.

Ships were lost, even close to home off Great Orme's Head at Llandudno, Balfour feeling twinges of guilt at his comfort at home while the men suffered for a pittance of a pay packet. He founded the Duke Street Home to provide better conditions for them, even buying up ale-houses and converting them into cocoa-rooms. He sent most of the sailors' wages to their homes to prevent their squandering it all as soon as they left the ship.

He was a member of the Town Council, he helped the poor and fought against the evils of drink. A lifelong Presbyterian, he died on 16th. April 1886 after an operation for the removal of a tumour.

The statue is by A.Bruce Joy and was cast in 1889 by H.Young & Co., Art Founders of London. It was erected by public subscription and was unveiled on 15th.November 1889 by the Rev.Canon Ellison in the presence of the Mayor, Bishop and others. The inscription tells us that "his life was devoted to God in noble and munificent efforts for the benefit of sailors, the education of people and the promotion of all good works."

Arthur Bower Forwood, Bart.

Arthur Forwood, born 1836, was educated at the Liverpool College under the Rev.Dr.Howson, Dean of Chester. He was good at mathematics, which was to stand him in good stead for his future career. Having finished his studies he joined his father's firm of merchants, Leech, Harrison & Forwood. Such was his drive that in 1861, aged only 25, he not only founded the West India & Pacific Steamship Co., but, in 1873 even took over his father's firm! Meantime, in 1871, he had been elected as Conservative councillor for North Toxteth, a post which he held until his death in 1898, also serving as Vice-Chairman of the Health Committee. Never stuck for a word, he was actually described as an over-active orator!

Eventually, Alderman Forwood became Mayor from 1877-8 and in this year he founded the Diocese of Liverpool and the University College of Liverpool. He was Chairman of the Cathedral Executive Committee and is commemorated in the Cathedral by an inscription in the wall below the organ. Strangely, he opposed the Lake Vyrnwy reservoir scheme without which Liverpool would be in a mess today. In 1885 he became M.P. for Ormskirk, a position which he held until his death, and by 1892 he was a Privy Councillor. He married twice, to Lucy Crosfield and later to Mary Eliza Baines. As if he didn't have enough to occupy him, he was Secretary to the Admiralty from 1886-92. He died in 1898, having lived a full and useful life.

His statue was executed by George Frampton in 1903 and unveiled by Lord Derby on July 21st, of the following year. It was "erected by the citizens of Liverpool in grateful recognition of the labours of a strenuous and self-sacrificing life devoted to the best interests of the Municipality and Port". He was "ernest and indomitable, endowed with great talents freely given to the public service. A leader of men."

Fig.16- Arthur B.Forwood

T.Major Lester

Born on 26th.August 1829 in what was then the country village of Fulham in London, Lester was educated at Newcastle-under-Lyme, King's College London and Christ's College Cambridge. He had a thirst for knowledge, but not for academic subjects like Latin, more for general ones like Literature. He spent a lot of his spare time exploring the British Museum and playing the organ.

He and his two brothers all chose the Church of England as their profession, Major Lester being ordained at Chester Cathedral in 1852, following which he served as curate at St.Barnabus in Parliament Street. The following year found him, as curate at St.Mary's Kirkdale, under the Rev.Dover. His dedication to his work must have impressed the parishioners because, after only one year there, they held a presentation evening for him, during which speeches were made in his honour. Rev.Dover was particularly impressed by Lester's dedication to the needs of the poor, especially as he had left behind him a life of luxury in Fulham.

Rev.Dover died in 1855 and it was the wish of himself and of the parishioners that Major Lester take over as Vicar in his place, which is what happened. Lester was there to witness history in the making as the city rapidly extended its boundaries, fine houses being demolished, squalid streets and courts being built in their place to house the thousands of workers and immigrants from Ireland who laboured in the docks and factories thereabouts. On 27th. June 1855, Lester married Elizabeth Maddock who was to be his wife for nearly 50 years

and was to bear him ten children, five of whom survived. She was a real lady of which the parishioners were extremely proud.

Lester's eloquent preaching held his congregations spellbound; his sermons on the evils of sin, the duty of prayer and the keeping of the Sabbath filling his church, even 48 years later when most churches were sparsely attended. From 1856 he started to help the poor by establishing a mission room, to be called the Kirkdale Ragged Schools. By 1860 he had founded the Kirkdale Child Charity and had scrounged the site and money for his first proper school in the street that was to be named after him. The foundation ceremony was attended by the dignitaries of the time.

In these schools poor children were fed, clothed and taught crafts and trades. To finance his projects, Lester wrote literally thousands of begging letters, all in his erratic handwriting, once spurning the offer of a typewriter from Sir.Alfred Jones as he just didn't have the time to learn how to use it! It was conservatively estimated that during his lifetime he raised at least £1 million for his charities! In 1864 he opened a home for girls in Walton Road, by this time having gained the nickname of "Old Blowhard" because of the way he used to blow out his cheeks as he walked along. He was Founder and Chairman of the Stanley Hospital Committee, the hospital being built on land given by Lord Derby in 1871, but it was always a struggle for funds to keep it open. He was made an Honorary Canon in 1884.

Always interested in education, he was Chairman of the Liverpool School Board from 1891 to 1903 and believed in the churches running their own schools despite the existence also of the council schools.

Fig.17- T.Major Lester

Despite his dedication to his work, he took a holiday each year, usually a cruise, courtesy of the shipowners, visiting the Holy Land, Mediterranean, Scandinavia, New York and many other places, usually accompanied by his piano!

His later years were dogged by chronic asthma and eventually he couldn't even manage the steps outside his house, having to make his way in through a special entrance. He died on Nov.3rd.1903, his last words to his wife being "You are a good woman". He was buried on Nov.7th. at Anfield Cemetery amid "scene of indescribable pathos". The funeral was attended by 50,000 people including many Catholic boys from Father Nugent's homes and representatives of all creeds and politics. The statue that we see here cost £1500, a large sum in those days, but a third of it was raised by door-to-door collections from folk who could little afford to give money away.

Unfortunately, nobody could match such a man and, after his death and without his genius for relieving the merchants of a few pounds, the flow of donations dried up and the homes closed, although the Education Committee took over his schools. In his lifetime, it is estimated that Major Lester cared for 10,000 children with about 14,000 going through his schools which at their peak were educating 2,700 pupils at one time. It gave him great pleasure when rich businessmen would come up and introduce themselves as having started life as "one of his boys", having made good from humble beginnings, thanks to him.

The statue was made by Geo.Frampton R.A. in 1907, bearing the inscription "Give the child a fair chance". It reminds us that Lester was "Vicar of St.Mary's, Kirkdale, for 50 years, honorary Canon of Liverpool, Rural Dean of Liverpool North and last Chairman of the Liverpool School Board". "He was loved by all, because he showed love to all ", "He was a pioneer in founding homes and schools where destitute children could be fed, clothed, educated and started in life, and he worked enthusiastically for them to the end of his days". The statue was "erected by citizens of all classes, creeds and parties" and was unveiled by Lord Derby on May 25th. 1907.

Father Nugent

James Nugent was born in Hunter Street, behind the Museum, on 3rd.March 1822 and baptised on St.Patrick's Day at St.Nicholas's Church, Copperas Hill. His father sold fish and poultry from his stall in St.John's Market, eventually the family living in Commutation row and, even later, in Crosby.

In 1838, James went to St.Cuthbert's College, Ushaw, Durham, and in 1842 to the English College in Rome. It is strange to think that during his early years he saw the first ever train leave for Manchester and the first steamship to cross the ocean from the Mersey.

After only three years in Rome, he was called home to be ordained by Bishop Brown on 30th.August 1846 at St.Nicholas's which was by then the Pro-Cathedral. There was, at this time, a drastic shortage of priests which neccessitated his early return from Rome, his first appointment being at St.Alban's, Blackburn.

The Irish famine of 1847 brought thousands of refugees flooding into Liverpool, only to add to the misery of those already living in filth and squalor, 300,000 arriving that year alone. Diseases, including Typhus, raged in the slums, thousands dying including many of the visiting clergy, later to be known as the Martyr Priests.

27,128 people were living in 14,085 cellars, in 5,841 of which lay pools of stagnant water, the children in some of them actually playing in the straw beside blackening stinking corpses.

At this time, Father Nugent went to St.Mary's in Wigan, but in 1849 returned to Liverpool as curate at St.Nicholas's and, miraculously, survived the rigours and dangers of the slums while his collegues perished. His love of the poor seems to have stemmed from his childhood when he had witnessed his mother helping so many people in distress. His brother, John, then went to Ushaw, was eventually ordained and founded the parish of the Blessed Sacrament in Walton, the foundation stone of that church being laid on 9th.July 1876 by the then R.C. Bishop of Liverpool, the Right Rev. Dr.O'Reilly.

Fig.18- Father James Nugent

At this time Catholic schools were almost unknown and, unbelievably, James Nugent had begun his education in a non-Catholic school! Determined to amend this state of affairs, he raised funds, bought a site in Hope Street and only six months later, on 31st. August 1853, Liverpool had its first sight of a Cardinal when none other than Cardinal Wiseman came to open the new school. Father Nugent was concerned at getting the children off the streets and out of mischief, was an advocate of compulsory education and was eager to have controls enforced over juvenile street-trading. He became involved in the setting-up of other schools, a matter he considered of some urgency especially when it was estimated that there were 23,000 children running loose around the dockside area alone! He realised that, amongst the starving thousands, there was so much talent going to waste that, in 1854, he actually got together with leading citizens of the day, including the Rev.Dr.Mc.Neill, a leading Orangeman, to try to get things moving under the slogan of "Save The Child". Today the citizens of Liverpool can see the wonderful friendship and co-operation between the Anglican Bishop and the Catholic Archbishop, but what an achievement it was on Father Nugent's part to encourage religious unity in those bigoted days in which he lived!

Getting the children into the schools was one thing, but after hours the waifs had to live in shop doorways and fend for themselves, no help being offered from the Government of the day which was strongly anti-Catholic. Night refuges were set up in which all creeds were catered for, an act which greatly endeared Father Nugent to all. Members of other religions would be referred to their own helpers the following morning, but not before they had been given a night's rest and shelter.

Fig.19- Father Nugent's Memorial at Ford Cemetery

Father Nugent was a great supporter of the Temperance movement and organised The League of The Cross which pursued this ideal. He also bought The Northern Press, now known as The Catholic Times. He was chaplain to Walton Jail for 22 years favouring long sentences as a way of ensuring a definite break with a prisoner's bad ways, rather than slipping back into them after a short respite. He helped to find homes for ex-prisoners in which they could work for their keep, many eventually going out into the Empire and making good for themselves. In July 1864 the Admiralty lent him an old ship, The Clarence, originally launched

in July 1827, to be used as a training ship on which the boys were taught various skills, especially reading and writing. The skills enabled many of them, ultimately, to find employment in the Merchant Navy. This venture was very successful until 17th.Jan.1884 when the ship was burnt out by the boys. After a lot of effort, and what we would now term "creeping", Father Nugent acquired a new "Clarence", but even this was deliberately burnt out by the boys after a systematic campaign of smuggling

Fig.20- Close-up of Father Nugent's Memorial at Ford

inflammable material aboard bit by bit.

Not content with close horizons, Father Nugent set sail for the U.S.A. on 18th.Aug.1870 with 24 orphan children to see if he could help them on their way in the New World. He found good homes for them all without difficulty, and then toured the U.S.A. and Canada for nine months, making many more such tours in the following years. It was a great joy to him, on his later visits, to meet his "old boys", now wealthy businessmen, who would eagerly present him with cheques to help him to help others like themselves. Although most of his work was in helping boys, he also helped "fallen women" and their illegitimate children.

On 19th. July 1904, King Edward VII and Queen Alexandra came to Liverpool to lay the foundation stone of the Anglican Cathedral, and Father Nugent was one of the welcome and honoured guests at the grand banquet at the Town Hall later in the day. Later that year, now aged 82, he was off to the U.S.A. again, but the travelling of those vast distances took their toll. Having covered that country myself on frequent occasions by bus, train and plane, I can appreciate just how gruelling it must have been on the transport of the day! Following a spell of recuperation at Hot Springs Virginia, he returned home aboard the Oceanic, but fell badly during a storm, banging his head.

He was now living in Formby but travelled frequently to Liverpool, partly to keep in touch with events but also to see his occulist for treatment of a sight impairment caused by his accident on board ship. On one of these visits he caught a chill which developed into pneumonia, from which he died at 4.00 am on 27th.June 1905, aged 83.

The funeral was held at the Pro-Cathedral the following Friday, the procession moving through the crowded streets in pouring rain, almost as if Heaven itself was weeping at the people's loss of their great friend, echoing the feelings of Catholics and Protestants alike. All the way to Ford Cemetery the route was lined by mourners three or four deep. The beautiful memorial over his grave at Ford is in the form of St.Vincent de Paul succouring the children, surely a fitting monument to a wonderful man whose talents and ideals would be welcome, even today in our so-called affluent society.

The statue, in St.John's Gardens, was erected by public subscription and was executed by F.W.Pomeroy. It was unveiled by Mr.R.D.Holt on 8th.Dec. 1906 amid much ceremony. The inscriptions around the base tell the story in concise terms: "Save The Boy", "His words: Speak a kind word. Take them gently by the hand, Work is the best reforming and elevating power; loyalty to country and to God". The rear side says "An eye to the blind, a foot to the lame, the father of the poor" and the right side,. "The Apostle of Temperance, the protector of the orphan child, the consoler of the prisoner, the reformer of the criminal, the saviour of fallen womanhood, the friend of all in poverty and affliction." The statue is believed, on good authority, to be the only one in a public place to commemorate a Catholic priest.

Father Nugents's name is still not forgotten because, in recent years, a new High School was named after him in Overbury Street in respect of such a great man.

William Ewart Gladstone

William Gladstone, born on 29th. Dec 1809 at 62, Rodney Street, was educated at Eton and Oxford where he soon became well known for his brilliant brain and dazzling oratory. Though he was a financial genius, his favourite subjects were religion and politics. A member of the Liberal party, he was first elected to Parliament in 1833, aged only 23! He soon made a name for himself, tireless in body and brain, working 16 hours a day, in each of those hours doing the work that would take any normal man four hours. He married in 1839, moving to the estate of his affluent wife at Hawarden, where he led a happy life with his collection of beloved books, his children and friends.

He had a room made to house his library which he called his "Temple of Peace" where he would study and unwind. His favourite hobby was tree-felling so maybe it's a good thing that he spent so much time in politics, otherwise the Hawarden countryside would soon have been rather bare!

As a direct contrast to this quiet pastoral life, once in Parliament, he set his listeners on fire with the eloquence of his powerful and fact-filled speeches. He won the admiration of both sides of the house as thy listened, spellbound, to his voice. His pet subjects were finance and colonial affairs, 1834 seeing him established as Lord of the Treasury and the following year in a post with responsibility to the colonies. Then the Liberals were voted out, but in 1841 he was back as Vice-President of the Board of Trade and then Chancellor of the Exchequer. His aim was to reduce the cost of living and, by skilful financial moves, was able to raise enough money in various ways so that he could repeal the hated Corn Laws which had levied a tax on imported grain, thus putting it out of reach of the pockets of the poor people. Incredibly, he actually decreased taxes and filled the treasury's coffers at the same time and, by 1868, as undisputed leader of the Liberals, was elected as Prime Minister. His laws opened up the Universities to men of all creeds, which had not been the case before, and he allowed official posts to be filled by those who had the ability and not just the influence in the right places.

Fig.21- The plaque outside 62, Rodney Street

The Irish were helped by the introduction of laws aimed to alleviate their suffering at the hands of absentee landlords and, always a champion of the poor, he passed laws to give the vote to more of the lower classes who could now vote in secret. Even Gladstone's good deeds, though, couldn't prevent his party being voted out in the elections of 1874. In moved his bitter rival, Disraeli with his Tories so

Gladstone left them to it, setting off to retire at his country idyll in Hawarden. But Disraeli's policies so angered him that he just couldn't settle down at home. Disraeli, more of an aristocrat, was prepared to back up the Turks in their quarrel with Russia, even to the point of going to war to help them. Gladstone embarked on what was, in effect, a one-man election campaign, so rousing the Country against Disraeli that, in 1880, he was back once again as Prime Minister, 70 years old and as lively as ever!

This next 5-year term of office produced the Reform Bill of 1884, giving the vote to even more people, but then the Tories were back in power, but only for a year! In 1886, and aged 76, Gladstone was back yet again as Prime Minister for his third term of office, albeit only of a year's duration this time.

He tried to get a bill passed which would have given home rule to Ireland but it failed through insufficient support. Following six more years of Tory rule, Gladstone returned once again for his fourth and final term of office as Prime Minister, by now having acquired the nickname of "The Grand Old Man", and not surprisingly so! This time he managed to get the Irish Home Rule Bill through the Commons, only for it to founder in the Lords. Finally, feeling his age, he retired to his home where he died on 19th.May 1898, a long and busy life at an end in a place which he loved so much. He is buried in Westminster Abbey.

Hawarden had, by that time, become a place of pilgrimage. Special trains and coaches would bring groups from far and wide to walk through the grounds of Hawarden Castle in the hope of seeing the great man who would sometimes come out and make an appearance to tumultous applause, the Village, meanwhile, doing a roaring trade in souvenirs!

It was no secret that Queen Victoria disliked Gladstone's stony approach and enjoyed the company of his rival, Disraeli, who was quite a charmer. In fact, the Queen never even called to see Gladstone on the one occasion that she happened to be in Hawarden. Nevertheless, he left a legacy to his country retreat, establishing St.Deniol's Library in the Village for the use of clergy, which is still in use to this day. His memorial in Hawarden Parish Church is well worth a visit and those interested can find more information available on the "Grand Old Man" there.

The monument in St.John's Gardens, one of most impressive there, is by T.Brock F.A.S. and was unveiled on 16th.July 1904 by the Rt.Hon.Earl Spencer K.G.. It cost £5,000, which was raised by public subscription, and is adorned with the figures of Justice and Truth with a plaque signifying Brotherhood affixed to the rear.

Fig.23- Gladstone Monument, Truth

Fig.24- Gladstone Monument, Justice

Fig.22- William Ewart Gladstone

Fig.25- Gladstone Monument, Brotherhood

William Rathbone and Agnes Jones

The general story of the Rathbones is given in the section on Sefton Park in which we look at William Rathbone the fifth. Here, in St.John's Gardens, we have the sixth of that name, born on 11th.Feb.1819 in Cornhill, Liverpool, in a spot where the Albert Dock Warehouse now stands. He was educated in Everton and at Heidelberg, following which he joined his father's firm which, at the time, was suffering rather a decline in its fortunes. Nevertheless, after becoming a partner in 1842, he began to build up the business dramatically by avoiding his father's specialisation in the American cotton trade. He traded with China and anywhere else he could, but eventually his main customers were in India and South America.

He instigated a system whereby he would build his ships in partnership with a number of friends, his first steamship being the "Memnon", the first of many to be built jointly for himself and Lamport & Holt, his business partners. When the first trans-Atlantic cable was laid, the Rathbones used it to signal grain prices to their New York office. Unfortunately, fraud at the cable company's offices made honest trading impossible as they wouldn't allow any forms of code to be used over their circuits. Eventually these problems were overcome but, by the 1870s, trade had suffered due to the fact that too many people were cutting profit margins to the bone as they chased the same markets.

Early in his career, Rathbone had decided to be a philanthropist, donating 10% of his earnings to charity, increasing the percentage as his earnings rose. As the years wore on he longed impatiently to devote more of his time to politics, education, religion and charitable works. The business had become very complicated and difficult to administer over such long distances and the advent of the steamship in large numbers had upset the balanced pattern of arrival of goods at the quayside. Their speed and capacity had resulted in excessive quantities of goods arriving all at once, causing a drop in prices and reduced profit. In essence, Rathbone appears to have got fed up with the firm and gave it to his partners who weren't very good businessmen anyway as they weren't sufficiently abreast of the times in an age where you had to think fast or go under.

From 1852 he organised the Liberal party in Liverpool, becoming its Chairman, but on 6th.Sept.1847, William had married Lucretia Gair, who died not long afterwards on 27th.March 1858. In his wife's last days she was attended by a nurse, a Mrs.Robinson, whose care and help so impressed Rathbone that he approached Florence Nightingale to ask how he could help to further the nursing profession in order that others may be helped. On the death of his wife, he kept Mrs.Robinson engaged in helping others at his own expense and between them they started a district nursing scheme, the first of its kind, soon to be copied by other cities around the country.

He built a Nurses' Home and, with £70,000 from Queen Victoria's Jubilee Fund, established Queen Victoria's Jubilee Institute for Nurses, nextdoor to the old Royal Infirmary. Under Agnes

Fig.26- William Rathbone VI

15

Fig.27- Rathbone VI Monument, District Nursing in the home

Fig.28- Rathbone VI Monument, Nursing in the Workhouse

Fig.29- Rathbone VI Monument, Education

Fig.30- Rathbone VI Monument, panel of facts

University, appealing for funds from Scottish merchants claiming that because their education was 50 years ahead of ours, it had enabled them to come here to make their fortunes! Having lead a full life, Rathbone died on 6th.March 1902, having served his city well. Unusually, the statue to him was made during his lifetime rather than posthumously as was normally the case. It was created by George Frampton in 1899 and, in the side panels, can be seen scenes depicting district nursing and education. Inscribed around the plinth we read that "Having faith in God, he could never despair of men", "seeing the best in others, he drew from them their best." "He deemed the fear of obstacles the greatest obstacle" and "he helped the poor by giving his heart with his help".

The statue was unveiled by the Lord Mayor, The Rt.Hon.Arthur Crosthwaite on July 26th.1901.

Agnes Jones, Rathbone's partner in the campaign to establish proper nursing in the workhouses, was only at Brownlow Hill workhouse for 2½ years before working herself to death, dying of typhus. Greatly loved by both inmates and staff, she lived from 1832 to 1868. The memorial illustrated is by Pietro Tenerani and actually represents an Angel of Resurrection because, although Rathbone wanted the figure to be of Agnes Jones, both her family and Florence Nightingale opposed the idea. The monument that we see here was placed in the Brownlow Hill workhouse until it was demolished in 1928 to make way for the Metropolitan Cathedral. It was then moved to the chapel at Walton workhouse, now Walton Hospital, where it was unveiled by the Lord Mayor, Margaret Beavan. Although the chapel is now a stores, the beautiful figure is still there, safe but unable to be enjoyed by the public. The inscriptions around the base are of great interest and are as follows.

Side one "In memory of Agnes Jones, daughter of Colonel Jones of Fahan, Ireland, who, under the auspices of the Liverpool Select Vestry, first introduced the system of trained nursing among the sick poor of a workhouse. In this service she lost her life. Her only desire for herself was that, at the Resurrection, her Lord might say: "She hath done what she could". "Born 10th.Nov 1832 Died 19th. Feb. 1868."

Jones, he introduced proper nursing for the inmates of the workhouses, other nurses being trained by her before being sent to other cities. In 1860 he had joined the committee of the Royal Infirmary, a plaque in his wife's honour being placed in the Nurses' Training School, now the Nurses' Home of that hospital. In 1862, the year that the school opened, he re-married, this time to Emily Lyle, his second cousin and Lady Superintendent of District Nurses. It was Emily who was responsible for starting the school nursing service. Rathbone was a member of Parliament for Liverpool and Caernarvon for many years. In 1878 he founded the

Fig.31- Agnes Jones Memorial, now in Walton Hospital

Side two. "She came to her Lord, offering to Him for His poor and sick, no sad and disappointed spirit, but the first fruits of her heart, in days when she was full of health and cheerfulness. She brought the world's sense and practical ability to God's work, and God's faith, hope and charity to the World's work, ernestly seeking the Saviour's spirit in following the blessed steps of His most holy life. She died at her post, among the poor and sick, while yet in the flower of her age, and thus she lived the life and died the death of the Children of God, who are the Children of the Resurrection. Florence Nightingale".

Side three.
"Alone with Christ in this sequestered place,
Thy sweet soul learned its quietude of grace.
On sufferers waiting in this vale of ours,
Thy gifted hand was trained for finer powers
Therefore,when Death,O Agnes, came to thee,
Not in the cool breath of the silver sea,
But in the City Hospital's hot ward,
A gentle worker for the gentle Lord.
Proudly as men heroic ashes claim,
We asked to have thy fever-stricken frame
And lay it in our grass, beside the foam
Till Christ the Healer calls his healers home"

The epitaph on Agnes.E.Jones's tomb at Fahan, Lough Swilly by the Bishop of Derry reads:

"The Master is come and calleth for thee", St.John XI.26

Agnes Jones is also commemorated in one of the Noble Women windows of the Liverpool Cathedral Lady Chapel.

King's Liverpool Regiment

This rather fine memorial is by W.Goscombe John A.R.A. and was placed here in 1905 to commemorate the dead of the Regiment in the wars of 1880-1902. For those keenly interested in the Regiment, a visit to the Museum opposite is a must, as there you will find an entire gallery and a small book devoted to the subject, but for the purposes of this book a potted history should suffice.

Incredibly, the origins of the Regiment date back to the time of the last battle to be fought on English soil. It was 1685, only 25 years after the first formation of a regular "army", and Catholic James II was on the Throne. James Scott, Protestant Duke of Monmouth, decided to take the Crown for himself and landed with an army of 82 men at Lyme Regis in Dorset from where he worked his way through various small towns as far as Wells.

To quell this uprising new regiments were formed, the "Princess Anne of Denmark's Regiment" being one of them, later to become the King's Regiment. Under the command of John Churchill, later to become Duke of Marlborough, Monmouth's campaign was halted at the Battle of Sedgemoor in July 1685. What the terrible weather and Churchill's men didn't do, the enthusiastic Judge Jeffries made up for. He had hundreds

Fig.32- King's Liverpool Regiment, rear of monument

hanged, drawn and quartered, burned or transported to Jamaica. The axeman had four goes at lopping off Monmouth's 27 year-old head, finally getting it off with his pen-knife!

After such an exciting start, the Regiment had a quiet time until 1715 when they gained the title of King's Regiment following heavy casualties in the Jacobite Rebellion. During the American Civil War they were involved protecting Canada from American invasion. The 1870s saw them in India during which time they made a record march of 770 miles which took them four months at an average speed of $2^1/_2$ m.p.h.! Service in Burma and at the North West Frontier followed but, despite deaths by injury, by far the greatest killer was disease. In fact, it was reported that, in Jamaica in 1742, nine out of every ten soldiers who died did so due to Yellow Fever. It was in 1881 that they became the King's (Liverpool) Regiment and, by the end of the century, were off to South Africa to fight the Boers. These were battles where many lessons were learned, three VCs won and a war in which the first ever trench warfare was fought at Magersfontein, near Kimberley.

The memorial that we see here was unveiled on 9th.Sept.1905 by Field Marshal Sir.George White VC. After noble service in both World Wars, the Regiment amalgamated with the King's (Manchester) Regiment in 1958, only to be disbanded at a special service at Liverpool Cathedral on 12th.March 1967, although the King's Regiment itself still survives.

Fig.34- King's Liverpool Regiment, top figure

King George III

Fig.35- King George III statue

In Monument Place is to be found this fine statue which is, in fact, on a spot once occupied by the house of a certain Polly Tittle. Originally designed to stand in Great George Square in what is

Fig.33- King's Liverpool Regiment, Detail of monument

now Chinatown, the foundations were laid there on 25th.October 1809 but, unfortunately, the enthusiasm of the general public at donating towards the cost of the proposed edifice was mild to say the least! By the time that the figure had been made and paid for, it had already been decided to position it on the site which it has occupied from 30th.Sept. 1822 to the present day.

A legend has it that the sculptor forgot to give the King stirrups in which to rest his feet and committed suicide in shame but, happily, Sir.Richard Westmacott R.A. lived on to the ripe old age of 81, dying in 1856 of natural causes!

In fact the statue, apart from the head, is a copy of one of Marcus Aurelius in Rome in whose time stirrups hadn't been invented. The inscription on the base reads "In Commemoration of the 50th. Anniversary of the Accession of His Most Gracious Majesty King George III to the Throne of These Realms."

Sea Circle, Seymour Street

Created by Charlotte Mayer in 1984, "Sea Circle", or "The Orange Peel" as it came to be called, was briefly the centre of a storm of controversy regarding its £15,000 cost.

Fig.36- Sea Circle

It was commissioned by the old Merseyside County Council to "humanise" the new road junction at the rear of Lime Street Station. Quite an emotive issue at the time, it has now been quietly accepted and forgotten.

Personally, I think that it's great, giving much scope for interesting photography. The attached plaque tells us that "This shell-like form embodies Merseyside's strong links with the sea. Its spiral is a symbol of outward growth and inward return. It reflects the constant coming and going of men, women and ships to and from this great port".

Eleanor Rigby, Stanley Street

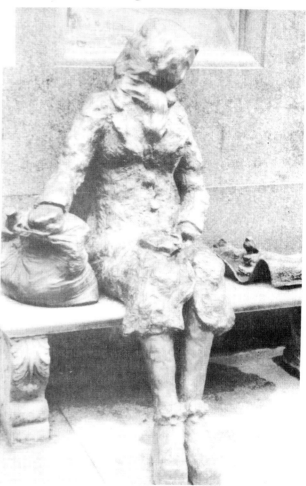

Fig.37- Eleanor Rigby

Donated to Liverpool by Tommy Steele for "half a sixpence", this figure shows the other side of this marvellous man's talents.

A total perfectionist, Tommy's stage shows are a joy to behold and I think that Liverpool should feel honoured to have received such a gift from a man who is proud to be a true Cockney yet can have such an affection for this Northern city. The plaque dedicates Eleanor "To all the lonely people" and was donated as a tribute to the Beatles. The casting was sponsored by the Liverpool Echo in December 1982.

C.G.Jung, Mathew Street

Fig.38- C.G.Jung

"Liverpool is the pool of life " said Mr.C.G.Jung in 1927. Well, we can't disagree with him as his statue peers out of the wall at the passersby in Mathew Street but, why he said it, I don't know.

Jung, born in 1875 in Switzerland, was the founder of Analytical Psychology. A contemporary of Freud, they eventually had to part ways professionally, Freud believing that all our actions are motivated by sex, whereas Jung claimed that we are more influenced by the accumulated memories of the preceding generations of our families. It was Jung who first presented the concept of introversion and extroversion. I found out more about his work but, as I didn't understand a word of it myself, I didn't think that the average reader would either so I left it out! Jung died in 1961.

Queen Victoria

At the corner of Lord Street and Castle Street can be seen this colossal monument to the great Queen of the world's greatest Empire. Wartime photographs show this structure as virtually the only survivor in a total wilderness of destruction, the stern-faced Queen looking, as if in defiance, on acres of buildings reduced to rubble by the German bombs.

The site was first used for the building of Liverpool Castle around 1235, the chequered history of which can be read about elsewhere. By 1721 the castle was totally ruined and was removed, to be followed by St.Georges Church which was built there in 1734. This was the church in which the Council members traditionally worshipped, all occupying their own pews, until one dreadful Sunday when the vicar, the Rev.James Kelly, preached an extremely anti-Jewish sermon inspired by the election of Jewish man Charles Mozley as Mayor. The obvious acute embarrassment spurred the Council worshippers to move to St.Peter's in Church Street. The subsequent decline in the fortunes of St.George's resulted in its eventual closure in 1887 and demolition two years later.

At 6.35 p.m. on 22nd.Jan.1901, Queen Victoria died at Cowes in the Isle of Wight. Once the news reached Liverpool, theatres and meeting places were closed, church bells tolled and the city was plunged into the deepest mourning. It was the end of an age as well as the beginning of a new century. The funeral took place on 2nd.February, there being held in Liverpool a memorial service and a procession in which the Lord Mayor, dignitaries and branches of all the civil and military services proceeded from the Town Hall to the Pro-Cathedral of St.Peter's in Church Street. The Non-conformists held their service in St.George's Hall and a day of more heartfelt and solemn mourning was never known in Liverpool. On 7th.March it was decided that a

Fig.39- Queen Victoria Monument

suitably magnificent monument be erected to honour the late Queen. The following year, Edward VII was crowned and, on 11th.Oct. of the same year, Earl Roberts laid the foundation stone of this monument which was completed in 1906 and unveiled on the 27th.Sept of that year by the Princess Louise, Duchess of Argyll. Apparently, the Princess was a sculptress herself and didn't think too much of her mother's likeness, although King Edward liked it.

The architects were Professor F.M.Simpson and Messrs. Willink & Thicknesse, the sculpture by Professor Charles J.Allan who executed it between 1902 and 1906. At one time there was a magnificent and spotless gents' toilet below the monument, recently removed, yet there is still said to exist an underground tunnel that once led from the castle to the bottom of James Street, the original tideline before decades of land reclamation. The patterns in the brickwork surrounding the monument are of an international-award-winning design and are supposed to represent the old ramparts of Liverpool Castle.

The monument is liberally decorated with sculpture of the highest quality, the photography of which has been extremely difficult, to say the least, as it is all black and in awkward locations. The rear elevations of the four sets of figures around the base are just as interesting as their fronts, so both are shown. It is thought that the faces on these figures are those of actual businessmen of the day.

The lower figures represent Agriculture, Commerce, Education and Industry while the upper ones are Wisdom, Justice, Charity and Peace, the four virtues of the Queen. Atop the dome stands the figure of Fame.

The Agriculture group can be seen holding a scythe, shepherd's crook and other farming items.

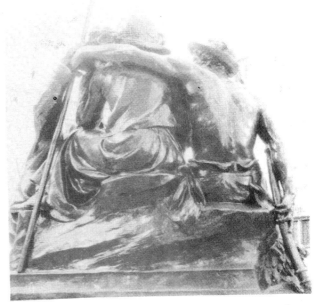

Fig.41- Queen Victoria Monument, Agriculture, rear view

In Commerce, one man carries his bag of goods, looking over a businessman's shoulder who, in turn, looks away from his ledger to inspect a model of his latest ship.

Fig.42- Queen Victoria Monument, Commerce, front view

Fig.40- Queen Victoria Monument, Agriculture, front view

Fig.43- Queen Victoria Monument, Commerce, rear view

In Industry, we see the blacksmith seated on the anvil, on which is symbolically placed the governor from a steam engine. He wields his pliers, watched by his admirers who include a lady who could be holding a distaff around which is wound the cotton before it is fed into the spinning wheel.

Fig.46- Queen Victoria Monument, Industry, front view

Education features the Master and an elder student, leaning together on a globe, watching a gyroscope while the young boy loses himself in a book.

Fig.44- Queen Victoria Monument, Education, front view

Fig.47- Queen Victoria Monument, Industry, rear view

Fig.48- Queen Victoria Monument, commemorative plaque

Fig.49- Queen Victoria Monument, commemorative plaque

Fig.45- Queen Victoria Monument, Education, rear view

Fig.50- Queen Victoria monument, commemorative plaque

Fig.53- Queen Victoria Monument, Charity

Fig.51- Queen Victoria Monument, Wisdom

Fig.54- Queen Victoria Monument, Peace

Fig.52- Queen Victoria Monument, Justice

Fig.55- *Queen Victoria Monument, Fame*

Atlantic Tower Hotel

ATLANTIC TOWER HOTEL Thanks to Mr.Leonard, a neighbour of mine, I discovered two fine pieces of sculpture in this prestigious hotel. In the lobby can be seen Cormorants Diving, by Sean Rice, 1972. The lively Seagull sculpture in the yard is well worth inspection, although it isn't certain if it is by the same artist.

Fig.57- *Atlantic Tower Hotel, The Seagulls*

Fig.56- *Queen Victoria*

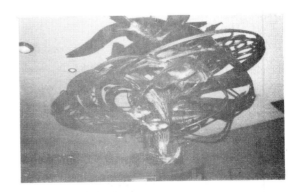

Fig.58- *Atlantic Tower Hotel, Cormorants Diving*

24

Exchange Flags

EXCHANGE FLAGS   Erected in 1924, this magnificent Exchange Newsroom war memorial by Joseph Phillips is worth detailed study. Stored for safe keeping during the last war, it was placed here in 1953. Civilian contributions to the war effort in the Second World War were marked by the addition of the figures of Mother and Child and Father and Child by Siegfried Charoux.

Fig. 61- Mother and Child

Fig. 59- Exchange Newsroom Memorial

Nelson Monument, Exchange Flags

Fig. 60- Father and Child

Fig. 62- Nelson Monument, front view

This monument to Lord Nelson was erected in 1813, eight years after his death and was Liverpool's first public sculpture.

Designed by Mathew Cotes Wyatt and modelled and cast by Richard Westmacott Jr., Nelson is seen with one foot on a cannon, the other on the dead body of an enemy. A flag, draped over his right shoulder, disguises the loss of that limb. The upturned sword in his left hand penetrates three crowns, representing his victories already won: St.Vincent, The Nile and Copenhagen. Victory herself is about to add a fourth crown for Trafalgar but, just as the battle is won, Death reaches out to touch Nelson on the chest.

A sailor rushes forward with a spear, representing the Navy's promise to avenge Nelson's death. To the rear, Britannia, leaning on her shield, weeps at the loss of this greatest of all naval heroes, a genius who had his officers in tears of admiration as he explained his proposed tactics for the battle of Trafalgar. His men needed no pressing to serve him; they revered him possibly because he, too, had human weaknesses, maybe enabling them to identify with him in some way.

The four chained figures around the base represent the four great victories of St.Vincent, The Nile, Copenhagen and Trafalgar. The four panels in the base depict scenes from some of Nelson's great naval actions. The grilles near these panels are to ventilate what used to be an underground warehouse, now a car park.

Although Nelson never came to Liverpool, he had intended to do so after Trafalgar, but the City had, in fact, made him a Freeman before that time.

Fig.63- Nelson Monument, rear view

Regarding the meaning of the four panels, I am deeply indebted to Mr.M.A.Nash of the Nelson Society for indentifying the scenes depicted.

Panel No.1: Nelson is seen here on the deck of the San Josef at St.Vincent on 14th.Feb.1797 receiving the Spanish swords. The sailor to the left who is holding a number of these swords reinforces the theory that this is the scene depicted here.

Fig.64- Nelson Monument, Panel No.1

Panel No.2: This appears to be representing Nelson's encounter with the Spanish gunboat off Cadiz later in 1797. A powerful scene.

Fig.65- Nelson Monument, Panel No.2

Panel No.3: It is thought that this is another scene from St.Vincent, showing Nelson receiving the sword from the dying Spanish Admiral.

Fig.66- Nelson Monument, Panel No.3

Panel No.4: Nelson is seen here fighting on land, but it is not known if it represents any actual occasion or is just symbolic of Nelson's bravery and devotion to his country.

Fig.67- Nelson Monument, Panel No.4

Simpson Fountain

Fig.68- The Simpson Fountain

This fountain, set into the wall of St.Nicholas's churchyard, commemorates William Simpson, owner of tea rooms on the landing stage in the last century.

In times of disaster he would place a large brass bowl where ferry passengers could drop in a contribution as they passed, the proceeds of which, over the years, helped the victims of famines, mining disasters and so on.

Simpson was anti-alcohol and a dedicated campaigner for the rights of the ordinary people. It is thanks to him that we have the public gallery in the Town Hall from which we can watch the Council meetings although this was only achieved following a sit-in and a subsequent ejection from the chamber!

The sculptor of this fountain was J.Rogerson and it was opened by Sir.James Picton on 10th.July 1885.

Fig.69- William Simpson

A determined attempt was made, in the early hours of a winter morning in 1989, to steal the stone lions from this monument. Fortunately, the police spotted three men struggling to move them across nearby Tower Gardens and were able to apprehend one of them. He was ultimately sentenced to six months in prison for taking the sculptures, estimated to be worth £500 each.

Engine Room Memorial

This interesting and wonderfully decorated memorial was erected in 1916 to those who really are the heroes of the sea both in war and peace, the engine-room men who work in heat, stink and noise in the very bowels of their ships. Without them, all would be lost. These poor men were always the last to get out in an emergency and were sometimes sealed in, left to certain death in a sinking ship as the watertight compartments were closed in order to maintain buoyancy.

Graphic accounts of the days of coal-fired ships describe the living hell of the stoke-hold, in which 5,000 tons of coal would have to be shovelled by hand into the insatiable furnaces to get a liner from Liverpool to New York.

Fig.70- *The Engine Room Memorial*

Fig.72- *The Engine Room Memorial, Officers*

Fig.71- *The Engine Room Memorial, Stokers*

Fig.73- *The Engine Room Memorial, Air*

28

The two stokers are seen standing before the furnace door, the higher-ranking men on the other side, presumably officers, stand beside the telegraph holding tools.

Higher up are depicted Air, Fire, Water and Earth. Sculpted by Goscombe John R.A., the work was originally intended to be the memorial to those lost on the Titanic in 1912, but its representation was extended to include all engine-room men lost at sea and is believed to be the only such memorial in the world.

The inscription reads: "The Brave do not die, their deeds live for ever and call upon us to emulate their courage and devotion to duty".

Fig. 76- The Engine Room Memorial, Earth

Fig. 74- The Engine Room Memorial, Fire

Fig. 77- Engine Room Memorial, Wreathed Propeller

Fig. 75- The Engine Room Memorial, Water

Fig. 78- The Engine Room Memorial, top Figures with Lifebelts

Merchant Navy Memorial

Fig. 79- The Merchant Navy Memorial

Fig. 81- Merchant Navy Memorial, Terrestrial Globe

The Merchant Navy Memorial at the Pierhead commemorates the 1,390 Merchant Navy men who were lost at sea during the Second World War.

The mirrored top to the column simulates a lighthouse lantern and the column itself is set at the centre of the points of a compass.

A globe of the world and one bearing the signs of the zodiac flank the entrance and are the work of H. Tyson Smith.

Edward VII

This imposing statue is the work of Sir. W. Goscombe John. R.A.

Fig. 80- Merchant Navy Memorial, Zodiac Globe

Fig. 82- King Edward VII Statue

Seven Seas

Fig.83- Seven Seas sculpture

In a small garden, between the bus station and the floating roadway, can be seen the Seven Seas sculpture designed by S.English and made by Bowman & Beddows.

In the next small garden can be found a stone plaque which reads: "Here in the dark days of war and in the dawn of victory, American troops and cargoes moved through this port, furthered by British and Americans working together. This stone records their unity in accomplishing their mission. Erected by the 15th-Port USA 1944".

Sir Alfred Lewis Jones

Alfred Lewis Jones, as his name may suggest, was a Welshman, born in Carmarthen in 1845. His association with Liverpool began with his education at the Collegiate School, followed by his initial career with Laird, Fletcher & Co., managers of the African Steamship Co.

He then traded on his own as a shipping and insurance broker until becoming, in 1879, partner in the Elder Dempster shipping line. By 1890 he was manager of the Elder Dempster & African Steamship Co., most of his business and interests being with West Africa, this trade becoming virtually monopolised by them shortly after Jones joined the firm. He established a college in Colwyn Bay for the training of Africans and was the principal founder of the Liverpool School of Tropical Medicine, recently extended and by no means redundant in this age of medical discovery.

Mainly due to his efforts, the banana trade was commenced, a side effect of this being the establishing of the Canary Islands and Jamaica as places of commerce and as health resorts. Earthquakes aren't very good for your health but, on one occasion in Kingston, Jamaica, Jones was there helping the injured after one of these disasters.

Jones had set up the banana industry by financing growers in the Canary Islands. In order to get the fruit here, he built the world's first refrigerated ship and, in 1901, still pioneering shipping innovations, built the first ship to be equipped with Marconi Wireless. He founded the

Fig.84- Sir.Alfred Lewis Jones Monument

Bank of West Africa, Elder Dempster eventually owning Britain's largest fleet of steamships. Some of the ships were so large that one of them was able to take 2,000 emigrants to Canada in one trip, another taking Boer prisoners to St.Helena!

Ever the big businessman, Jones would buy and sell whole companies, once selling the Beaver line, comprising fifteen ships, to the Canadian Pacific Railway Co.. Elder Dempster have been in the forefront of innovation in other ways, including the

Fig.85- Alfred Lewis Jones Monument, detail of front

first British shipping company to use air transport and to establish its own cadet training school.

It was Jones who brought the banana to the ordinary working man or, as it was said at the time, "to the masses as well as the classes". As was the case until fairly recently, our ancestors were wary of any strange foods and, in order to popularise his bananas, Jones employed a whole band of London costermongers for a year to sell the fruit in Lime Street in their own persuasive manner, the prices dropping as the day wore on.

In 1901 Jones was created a KCMG for his services to the colonies of Jamaica and West Africa. In politics he described himself as "progressive", but his main interest at home and at work was commerce. Another claim to fame is that he was instrumental in saving from destruction many of the trees in the southern part of the City, so that we may still enjoy many of them today.

Jones died at "Oaklands" in Aigburth on 13th.Dec.1909 and the monument, by Sir.George Frampton R.A., was unveiled on 13th. July 1913 by Lord Derby.

The face of Sir.Alfred is to be seen on the front, the top figure representing Liverpool and its shipping.

The Fruits of Industry on the left holds a variety of fruit, most of which the Elder Dempster ships would have carried. She also holds the Caduceus wand in her other hand, symbol of Peace and Commerce.

Research, on the right side, holds a microscope and a book. The rear panel shows a lovely sailing ship.

Fig.87- *Alfred Lewis Jones Monument,* Fruits of Industry

Fig.86- *Alfred Lewis Jones Monument, Liverpool and its Shipping*

Fig.88- *Alfred Lewis Jones Monument,* Research

Fig. 89- Alfred Lewis Jones Monument, detail of rear

Arthur Dooley

I thought it best to include some Arthur Dooley work for devotees of the ultra-modern. He seems to be at his best when creating figures in the religious vein, and this crucifix may be seen on the Methodist Centre at the corner of Princes Avenue and Arundel Street.

Fig. 90- Arthur Dooley sculpture

Florence Nightingale

At the corner of Princes Road and Upper Parliament Street can be seen the memorial to the great Florence Nightingale, carrying her famous lamp as she administered medication and compassion to the sick.

Fig. 91- Florence Nightingale memorial

She took her name from Florence in Italy, where she was born on 20th.May 1820. The years of her gentle upbringing in Embley, near Romsey in Hampshire, and later in Derbyshire, were when she gained a love of nature and it was in these same years that she began to get a feeling that she was destined to perform great deeds for mankind. She felt that she was wasting valuable time indulging in her idle society pursuits which were, indeed, the accepted life-style of a well-educated young lady of the time.

She was well-loved by her father's tenants on their country estate and, even then it appears, she exhibited a gift for healing because the story was told of how she set the broken leg of the shepherd's dog and saved its life after all others had given up hope. She studied quietly, becoming fluent in French, German and Italian. As if that were not enough to occupy her time, she gave Bible classes at home for young women of all faiths.

Those who met her found her charming and interesting but, in 1846, she wrote that "I feel that my sympathies are with ignorance and poverty". Her parents were shocked at her desire to take up the nursing profession as such a girl was not expected to mix with the un-trained, low-class drunken women of which the nursing fraternity was believed to be mainly comprised!

In fact, the only organised nursing body was a small training home run by the Quaker philanthropist, Mrs.Fry, whom Florence went to see. It was finally in 1850, on her thirtieth birthday, that she decided, in today's parlance, to do her own thing, not an easy decision to be made by a single lady in those days which were ruled by manners and protocol. In taking this decision she was casting aside the plans that her parents had made for her future and at least one good offer of marriage.

But, she had already toured foreign hospitals, including those of Egypt and so, with her eyes wide open, she entered a nursing institution in Kaiserwerth in Germany to receive her first formal training.

She now experienced, for the first time, a deep sense of fulfilment as she realised her desire to help the sick and needy. Upon leaving Germany she toured London, Edinburgh and Paris, studying the workings and faults of the various hospitals in those cities. It was in 1854 that, as superintendent of the "Hospital for Invalid Gentlewomen" also known as the "Home for Sick Governesses," she learned of our country's involvement in the Crimean War.

As the tales filtered back of the terrible conditions in the hospitals at the Front, Florence and her lifelong friend, Sidney Herbert, Secretary for War, decided that she should set out for Scutari, near Istanbul, with a group of 37 nurses to assist the French Sisters of Mercy who were struggling to cope.

She sailed on Oct.21st. to find a hospital in a condition so insanitary that it defied belief. Its maximum accommodation was 2,434 and it had four miles of beds only 18" apart filled with men deprived of proper food, comfort and cleanliness.

Incredibly she managed to superintend eight hospitals but, although she had been sent out by the Government, her biggest obstacle was that of officialdom, loath to accept this mere woman who seemed to know better than they.

She ended up in paying for many of the improvements herself, working day and night, eventually making herself ill as well. But, at least her efforts were not going un-noticed, her achievements acquiring her fame and influence.

She was admired by all, from the Queen down to the most humble citizen. One high official stated that "She has taught officers and officials to treat the soldiers as Christian men". Although there were some fanatics who criticised her on religious grounds for "trying to capture the souls of her patients", she was defended by the Queen and by the American poet, Longfellow, who immortalised her in verse:

So in that house of misery,
A lady with a lamp I see
Pass through the glimmering gloom,
And flit from room to room.
And slowly, as in a dream of bliss,
The speechless sufferer turns to kiss
Her shadow as it falls
Upon the darkening walls.
On England's annals, through the long
Hereafter of her speech and song,
A light its rays shall cast
From portals of the past.
A lady with a lamp shall stand
In the great history of the land,
A noble tye of good
Heroic womanhood.

Florence had set out to train her nurses to work to a discipline, and to administer the orders of the doctors. Though she was undoubtedly a firm leader, she was filled with compassion for her patients, visiting them long after the other nurses had retired for the night, maybe helping them to write home to their loved ones

Making her rounds at night, lamp in hand, she inspired hope and contentment in the minds of the suffering who would, as Longfellow states, kiss her shadow should it fall upon them, then sink back quietly in their beds, soothed by the inspiration of her presence.

In six months she reduced the death rate per thousand from 420 to 20! She spent some time at Balaclava, working herself into an illness that was to be with her for many years. She finished her war service back at Scutari, by now established as a National heroine. Streets, lifeboats and even race-horses were named after her but she returned home quietly, despite having been offered a tumultuous welcome. She worked unceasingly to better the lives of sick soldiers but the death, in 1861, of her dear friend, Sidney Herbert, was a great loss.

In her Crimean days, a Nightingale Fund had been started and this financed the training of nurses at St.Thomas's Hospital in London. It was her influence that helped in the formation of the Red Cross and she even involved herself with the sufferings of the people of India, being awarded the Order of Merit in 1907. Following her death on 13th.Aug.1910, she was buried in Embley beside her parents, despite her having been offered a tomb in Westminster Abbey. Her tombstone bears only the dates of her birth and death and the initials F.N.

It has been said of this lady, founder of nursing as we know it today, that she was "Florence Nightingale, the Angel of Pity, whose name will shine forever in letters of gold in the pages of history".

It was in 1859 that William Rathbone decided to set up a scheme whereby the sick could be treated in their own homes by skilled nurses. He asked the advice of Florence Nightingale in this matter and they remained friends from then on.

In 1862 a training school and home for nurses was founded at the Royal Infirmary, the training school itself being in charge of all the nursing work until 1897. A fund had been set up to commemorate the long reign of Queen Victoria, and it was decided that the proceeds of that fund be spent on improving the nursing service. Assistance was received from the David Lewis Trust who offered to build a new Central Home for the nurses at a cost not exceeding £10,000. It was felt that this was an appropriate time to re-organise the body and, on 8th.Feb.1898, The Liverpool Queen Victoria District Nursing Association was formed, representing interested bodies including the David Lewis Trust, the Northern and Southern Hospitals &c.. The whole city was divided into districts, a nurse for each..

Patients paid a small fee which was only a fraction of the cost of the service which was, in turn, supported by benefactors. Present District Nurses might be amused at the hours worked by their predecessors in those days: 8.30am until 1.00pm then off duty until 4.30pm when they would have tea following which, at 5.00pm, they would start their evening rounds! Twelve to twenty patients per day was the usual workload.

In 1902, William Rathbone died and his friend, Florence Nightingale, sent a wreath to be placed on his grave in remembrance of "One of God's best and greatest sons".

The Nursing Association building is adjacent to the Florence Nightingale memorial, the sculptor of which is given as Charles J.Allen, although H.Tyson Smith is thought to have worked on it as well, when he was working for Mr.Frank Norbury. Both the monument and the building were designed by William E. Willink.

The inscriptions on the memorial are as follows:

Left side: "This memorial was erected in 1913 by the citizens of Liverpool in gratitude to Florence Nightingale, strong of heart and undaunted by difficulties. She brought succour to the sick and wounded in the Crimea and taught the nations how the sufferings of war can be redeemed by mercy and heroism. In years of peace, by inspiration and guidance, she won for the vocation of the Nurse a place of honour in the National life".

Right side: "For fifty years the nursing institutions of Liverpool alike in workhouse hospitals, district and training homes found in her a friend and counsellor , ripe in experience, wise in judgement, unwearied in sympathy. To perpetuate her name, provision has been made for the maintenance of special nurses on the staff of the District Nursing Association."

Fig.92- Queen Victoria District Nursing Association

Hugh Stowell Brown

This statue, in Princes Avenue, by F.J.Williamson, commemorates Hugh Stowell Brown, born on 10th.Aug.1823 in Douglas I.O.M. where he stayed with his clergyman father until the age of fifteen.

He then moved to England with the intention of learning Land Surveying but, after two years of this he decided to try engineering at the London & Birmingham Railway's works at Wolverton. He stayed there until he was 21, by which time he had driven a railway engine from Wolverton to Crewe.

In his autobiography he describes many interesting facts and stories of the early days of the railways in 1840. Their routine differed somewhat from ours: he rose at 5.30am, walked a mile to work and then cooked his breakfast in the smith's forge! If this didn't take up enough of his waking hours, he managed to get a bit of spare time in which he studied Greek ånd other Classical languages, finally

deciding to follow family custom and enter the Church.

He returned to the Isle of Man to spend three years at King William's College during which time he began to have doubts on certain aspects of the doctrine of the Church of England, deciding that his niche in life lay in the Baptist Church. Incredibly, by 1848, aged only 25, he was Minister of Myrtle Street Baptist Chapel but, due to his popularity and magnetic personality, the church, which had only been built in 1844, soon became inadequate and, in 1859, had to be enlarged to seat congregations of up to 2,000 people!

He was a masterful preacher who knew his Bible inside out, holding the numbers of his congregation despite the general fluctuations in local population and changes in the habits of church-going. He was well-known for his Sunday-afternoon lectures to the working classes at the Concert Hall in Lord Nelson

Fig.93- Hugh Stowell Brown

Fig.94- Old Concert Hall, Lord Nelson Street

Street which he started in 1854, talking in plain language to anything up to 3,000 ordinary people at a time. He even toured the country lecturing on various subjects, his text always enlivened with his overflowing humour.

In 1873, he spent a very interesting 12 weeks in the USA and Canada. One thing that he found very puzzling was the widespread use of paid choirs in the churches over there, the congregations listening to them but not joining in! I suppose it was a case of "why have a dog and bark yourself!" He noted particularly the lack of drunkenness there in comparison with England.

His visit to Salt Lake City was an insight into a different world, that of the Mormon Church. He was amazed to see the bored congregations at the Mormon Tabernacle yawning and spitting as they waited for it to be over!

The flagrant display of polygamy disgusted him so much that he was only too glad to leave, just as a train load of 400 girls arrived from England to become new Mormon wives! He had noticed that most of the people that he had met there had originated from Britain and, despite their various collections of "better halves", they didn't seem very happy in what would sound to many an idyllic situation!

Brown was actually married twice himself, but only to one at a time! Strangely, both wives died before his own death on Wednesday 24th.Feb.1886

at 29,Falkner Square.

A lifelong pacifist, Brown was commemorated by the people that he loved, who erected this statue of him in the grounds of the Myrtle Street Baptist Chapel where it was unveiled by the then Mayor, Mr.E.H.Cookson on Oct.15th.1889. It was moved to a site in Princes Avenue in September 1954 but, in June 1988, it was pulled over and damaged by vandals and is at present in storage. For those more interested in the life of this notable man, I can recommend Hugh Stowell Brown's autobiography, edited by W.S.Caine, in the Central Library.

Stowell Street, Liverpool 7, is named after Hugh Stowell Brown.

Abercromby Sq

The monolith with two holes to be seen in the square is, in fact, the only example, as far as I know, of a Barbara Hepworth sculpture to be seen outdoors in Liverpool.

Born and educated in Wakefield, Dame Barbara was soon off to commence her artistic studies in Italy. She spent most of her happy working life in St.Ives where she died in a fire at her studio aged 72 on 20th.May 1975. The studio is now a museum to this talented and lavishly honoured lady who changed from the orthodox style of work to this abstract mode around the time of the birth of her three sons in late 1934.

Senate House, the modern building adjacent, was completed in 1968 and it would appear that the sculpture was placed here at that time.

Fig.95- *Abercromby Square, Barbara Hepworth Sculpture*

Minster Court

In the garden of what was once a Council block of Thirties flats, is to be seen this exceptionally fine pair of figures by Sean Rice. Appropriately entitled "Renaissance", it was unveiled by the Rt.Hon. Tom King MP., Secretary of State for the Environment, to commemorate the opening of what was by then known as Minster Court on 4th.March 1983. The buildings had been converted from a problem block into secure and desirable residences by Messrs. Barratt, builders.

Hannah Mary Thom

Although, sad to say, many of the monuments mentioned in this book have suffered at the hands of the lawless, the story of this one is refreshingly different. Once to be seen in the centre of nearby Standish Street, the poor figure was badly defaced and mutilated, parts going missing even as far back as 1928, when the word "vandal" was probably unknown. Luckily, she was rescued by the compassionate local priest of Holy Cross Church who secured her in the confessional where she was to languish in her battered state for many years.

Fig.96- *Minster Court, Renaissance*

Fig.97- *Hannah Mary Thom Statue*

It is to Mr.Miles Broughton, Chairman of the local Victorian Society, that we owe the eventual restoration. It was Miles who arranged funds for the restoration and placing of the figure on its plinth in the safe and pleasant grounds of Mazenod Court sheltered accomodation.

Quite a lot of the figure was missing but, working only from archive pictures, local sculptor Jim Mc.Laughlin was able to recreate the missing parts to perfection. The marble layer between the figure and the Aberdeen Granite base was perished with the action of rain on the copper and all of the original lead letters of the inscription had long since been stolen. It was decided that a new piece of stone be cut with the inscription engraved into it.

Hannah lived from 24th.Nov 1817 to 31st.Dec.1872 and was the second daughter of William Rathbone the Fifth, whose statue stands in Sefton Park. On 2nd.Jan.1838 she married John Hamilton Thom, Unitarian Minister at Renshaw Street Chapel, but they were to have no children. Rev.Thom founded the "Ministry of the Poor" in the same year, a charitable undertaking providing help and religion to all and operated from the North and South Domestic Missions.

Hannah was, until her death, Lady Superintendent of District Nurses in the Marybone area and it was the grateful poor who raised the cash to erect the fountain to the lady who had given selflessly of herself to help them in their suffering.

Cast by the Coalbrookdale company, the figure was sculpted by the Wills Bros. On the afternoon of Friday, 11th.Sept.1987, the fully restored statue was unveiled by Mr.R.S.Rathbone, yet another link with the great family who have, for so many years, been a vital part of the life of Liverpool.

Fig.98- West Derby Village, Drinking Fountain

West Derby, The Fountain

The famous fountain was the gift, in 1894, of Richard Robert Meade-King and was designed by Arthur P.Fry. Patterns of fish can be seen and also the motto "Water is Best", a rather cheeky inscription as the fountain is within sight and staggering distance of three pubs! Maybe it was one of the landlords who made sure that the water doesn't run any more!

Richard Robert Meade-King was born on 20th.June 1850, son of Henry Warren Meade-King, JP for Lancashire and Liverpool and resident of Sandfield Park, West Derby. Richard had a private education followed by studies at London University College, after which he entered the world of commerce, initially at a firm of general brokers, Cox Brothers.

Later, he joined a Mr.J.F.Robinson, forming a partnership in a firm which specialised in dealing with petroleum, surely an unusual commodity in those days! He entered the world of politics, becoming the Liberal councillor representing St.Paul's ward from 1891 and for many years after that.

He was noted for his smart dress, usually attired

Fig.99- Meade King, from 1894 Liverpool Review

in a dark red tie with diamond pin, turned-down collar, steel pebble glasses, his hair roughly centreparted. He rarely spoke in the council chamber and then only in a quiet way, rather unlike the debates of today!

He served on three committees: the Health Committee, Parks, Gardens and Improvements Committee and the Library, Museum and Arts Committee. He was extremely well-read, well-travelled and cultured. He strove to improve the condition of the masses, not by the traditional Socialism of the time involving the fair-shares-of-wealth ideal, but by the improvement of the amenities available to the ordinary folk in the hope that this enrichment of their lives would do them just as much good by improving their life style and leisure hours.

He was asked if, in his opinion as a well-travelled man, there was a likelihood of the Continental Sunday eventually becoming the norm. in this country whereby more premises would be open for trade and so on, as was the case in Paris. He doubted that any change in our habits was likely and that we should carry on enjoying our leisure and recreation on Sundays rather than indulging in more work. He must have been a very far-sighted man as,

even to this day, Sunday is still mainly a day of leisure.

His aim was parks, pictures, books and music for the ordinary people to enjoy. He was a long-standing member of the Liverpool Kyrle Society, founded to help the aged, poor and sick. He was active in the "Trees and Seats Dept." of the Society for many years, providing these amenities in various open spaces in the city.

By 1930, he was a Liberal Alderman and it was in March of that year that he entered the debate to decide the fate of Tue Brook Cottage at the bottom of Millbank. The cottage had been built in 1615 by John Mercer, a yeoman farmer, and it was proposed to demolish it to make way for two new houses, the area being rapidly built up at that time with Council homes.

Meade-King led the campaign to save the cottage and, thanks to him, it still stands today, the oldest Council house in the city and one of the oldest inhabited houses in Liverpool.

Despite an attack of Typhoid fever in 1893 which left him prematurely aged, Richard lived to a ripe old age, dying in 1934, having witnessed many changes both architectural and social, but always a true friend to his native West Derby.

Fig.100- Tue Brook Cottage, Millbank, Tuebrook

West Derby, The Monument

Ask anyone in West Derby who is the figure seated at the top of the Monument and they will probably say that it is Queen Victoria, so brain-washed are we to believe that the great Queen inhabits every monument in the land! In this case, she had to make way for Jesus, sitting there with his Bible. The difficulty is that the only time of the year that His face is well illuminated beneath the canopy is when the sun is shining almost horizontally at the time of the shortest days of Winter, appropriately at Christmas time.

Is it pure coincidence, we may wonder, that at only this appropriate time of the year is Jesus's face illuminated or is it a clever piece of design on the

part of Eden Nesfield, the creator of the monument? The mind is drawn to the famous two-mile-long Box Tunnel built on a slight incline by the great I.K.Brunel when he constructed the Great Western Railway. Was it again pure coincidence, or a measure of his genius, that there is only one time when the sun shines right through the tunnel, the days on or around his birthday? It is something to think about!

Although other parts of the edifice are rather eroded by wind, rain and pollution, Jesus's face is perfectly preserved in its layer of soot.

The Monument was erected by Mrs.J.P.Heywood of Norris Green to mark the

Fig.101- West Derby Village, The Monument

Fig.102- The Monument, the face of Jesus

Eve in the Temptation scene with the serpent wrapped around the Tree of Life, the Hand of God beckoning down from above.

St.Luke was a physician and is the Patron Saint of artists and doctors. He is shown with a cow or ox, probably referring to the Nativity scene, Luke being the one who describes the Virgin Birth in the greatest detail in the Bible. St.Mathew was a tax collector for the occupying Romans before joining Jesus and His disciples. He can be shown in various ways, but he is seen here sitting on what could be a money-chest, depository for his collected taxes.

St.Mark is usually symbolized by a lion, but here is seen only with a bird, reading his book.

St.John is patron of all those who work with books, but he is usually shown with his emblem, the Eagle. Virtue's Catholic Encyclopedia tells us that this is his symbol because, in his gospel, he rises high above the Earth and, like the Eagle for the Sun,

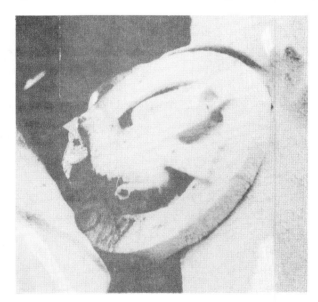

Fig.103- The Monument, Knowledge

position of the altar of the Ancient Chapel of West Derby which had stood there for over 500 years until its demolition in the years 1853-6 following the completion of the magnificent new church nearby.

The four saints. Mathew, Mark, Luke and John are to be seen at the top of the column, while behind Jesus are four doves encircled by rings in which are inscribed various virtues, so badly eroded now that only "Knowledge" and "Strength" can really be made out.

The rear of the Monument is quite elaborate, showing scenes of the Crucifixion and Adam and

Fig.104- The Monument, detail of rear

makes straight for the heart of the mystery of God. John understood Jesus more than anyone else and was very close to Him, so much so that he was the one who coined the expression "God is Love".

While all the other Apostles suffered death by martyrdom, John lived on to a ripe old age but, seeing his friends die off one by one, usually in some unpleasant way, he suffered what had been called "martyrdom of the heart", fittingly describing the anguish and loneliness that he must have felt toward the end of his life.

Fig.105- The Monument, St.Luke

Fig.107- The Monument, St.Mark

Fig.106- The Monument, St.Mathew

Fig.108- The Monument, St.John

Bowden Fountains

Intrepid voyagers, travelling on the 75 or 12 bus, out of the city, will pass these two fountains, the Frederic Bowden one near Brougham Terrace and the Thomas Bowden one at the top of Millbank, by Queens Drive.

The Frederic Bowden fountain was erected in 1913, the ironwork being by W.Mc.Farlane & Co. of Glasgow, there being originally a lion head as water spout. The Thomas Bowden fountain was donated in 1911 and is now almost completely wrecked, such a shame as it once stood in open countryside.

Frederic Bowden was born in 1825 in Tremington, North Devon. He came to Liverpool in 1843 and joined Boutcher, Bowden, Limington & Co., hide & leather merchants. Over the years, the firm's name was changed but he stayed with them until 1884.

He was very interested in the work of the Liverpool Dispensaries, joining their committee in 1871, and serving in various roles until he became president in 1900, holding also the post of Treasurer. He was to stay in this office until the day he died, having attended over 2,000 meetings!

Fig.109- Frederic Bowden Fountain

Fig.110- Thomas Bowden Fountain

Fig.111- Frederic Bowden Fountain, plaque

Fig.112- Thomas Bowden Fountain, plaque

He was also on the committee of the RSPCA from 1878 to 1894 and its Chairman from 1894 to 1903. His church was St.James's, West Derby, which he attended for 40 years. His wife, Eliza, bore him two children, Thomas and Eliza, and in 1909, Frederic and Eliza celebrated their Diamond Wedding. But happiness was short lived as Thomas died later that year and his mother died the following year, 1910. In February of 1910, at a meeting of the Liverpool Dispensaries, Frederic caught a chill from which he never really recovered, dying from its effects on Monday 1st.May 1911 aged 86. He was keen of mind and in full possesion of all his faculties to the end. His funeral was at St.James's and he was buried at Anfield Cemetery. He had lived a full life and a successful one, leaving £28,537 in his will.

Pity poor Eliza, his daughter, later to become Mrs.Hugh Mc.Cubbin, who saw her brother Thomas, mother and father all die within two years. It was she who donated the drinking fountains in their memory.

She lived at Millbank House, No.6, Millbank, but the original house is now gone. The family home survives though, "Fernside", 4, Haymans Green, West Derby Villlage, which is where Frederic lived.

Fig.113- Fernside,

4,Haymans Green,

West Derby

Knotty Ash

This interesting old village possesses many unusual features waiting to be discovered. Opposite the Knotty Ash Hotel stands the now "dry" drinking fountain with its cheeky inscription "water's best!" Dated 1887 it was donated by someone whose initials were E.T.

A little further along East Prescot Road can be seen the former Knotty Ash Brewery of Joseph Jones & Co., part of which was built as far back as 1884, and taken over by Higson's in 1927. In the windows of the nearby pub. can be seen some of the original windows depicting the Knotty Ash tree.

The obelisk, standing in Springfield Park, is a

Fig.114- Inscription in fountain

Fig.115- Knotty Ash, Drinking Fountain

Fig.116- Former Knotty Ash Brewery

Fig.118- The Lord Nelson Pub., near the Old Brewery

Fig.117- Nelson Obelisk, Springfield Park

Fig.119- Boundary Post, Thomas Lane/Thingwall Lane

Fig.120- Boundary Post, Thomas Lane, detail of top

monument to Lord Nelson, erected on what, at the time, was his own land by a Mr.Downward, sugar refiner.

Initially he offered the monument to the City, who declined it, thinking it unworthy of a place in their streets, even describing it as a "half Nelson!" So, Mr. Downward decided to erect it in the grounds of his house, Springfield. The tablet commemorating Nelson has gone, but he is, nevertheless, still remembered in the name of the public house right opposite!

At the corner of Thingwall Lane and Thomas Lane stands this interesting old boundary post inscribed "Road to Broadgreen" and "Road to Thingwell new Thoroughfare."

Thingwall, as it is called nowadays, would have been a place of Parliament in the days of the Vikings. Similarity exists with Iceland's Thingvellir and the Manx Tynwald, outdoor meeting places where laws are made.

Also on the post are the initials J.C. 1776. These were the initials of James Clemens, Mayor of Liverpool in that year who had a fine house opposite called Ashfield. He owned much local property and his house, now known as Thingwall Hall, still stands.

Before the First World War, the house was home to Henry Bright,who wrote a book "A year in a Lancashire Garden" based on his own estate which soon became famous and a source of both interest and admiration, drawing visitors from far and near.

Princes Park

The inscription on the obelisk in Princes Park reads "To the Memory of Richard Vaughan Yates, the Enlightened and Philanthropic Founder of Princes Park. Erected by Public Subscription 1858".

Richard Vaughan Yates was born in Everton on 4th.July 1785, son of the Rev.John Yates. The family were great lovers of art and books, part of their collection now forming part of the collection at the Walker Art Gallery. But it was the to the iron industry that Richard owed his wealth, finally retiring from it only two years before his death, having been the senior partner in the firm of Yates, Cox & Cox.

He gave much of his riches to aid the poor and deprived, being especially interested in the education of the under-privileged, many of whom attended the Harrington School in Stanhope Street, founded by his father (now demolished). In fact, for over thirty years, he not only funded the school but, when time permitted, got stuck in and did a bit of teaching there as well! Many folk will ease their concience by merely making a monetary donation, but few actually challenge a social problem head-on like this.

Although not heavily involved in politics, Yates found time to serve on the Town Council and to give his time as Magistrate but, unlike many politicians today, he tolerated his opponents charitably, earning himself a reputation of not having a single enemy either in the world of politics or that of religion, something that must stand as a record in itself!

He did not have the strongest of constitutions and occasionally travelled to the Mediterranean and Middle Eastern countries, partly as a rest-cure and partly out of intelligent curiosity.

During the months of May and June 1805, he took a tour of Wales and Ireland, entering Wales through Wrexham, travelling through Conway to Holyhead from where he crossed to Dublin. Returning through Anglesey to tour more of North

Fig.121- Richard Vaughan Yates Obelisk

Wales, he eventually saw the south of the Principality before returning home. So keen was he to sample every facet of the area that he even climbed Snowdon in order to witness the wonderful sight of the sunrise over the mountains.

His main reason for this tour of picturesque places was to enable him to build up a mental store of all the lovely scenes that he could recall and enjoy the memory of "in the intervals of business". Such a trip doesn't sound remarkable in our age of easy travel but, bearing in mind what the roads must have been like in 1805 before the age of the train or car, it must have been quite an exciting undertaking!

Yates wrote down his thoughts and experiences on this trip, expressing his love of the scenery, but also noting his abhorrence of the poverty and begging that he encountered, especially in North Wales. He found the South Wales people more affluent, but of those in the North he said that "people appear to be still in a state bordering on barbarism in their dress, their habitations and their manners, which are extremely rude". Nevertheless, the trip had a profound effect on him, opening his eyes to the joys of the open air, away from the crowded streets of the now rapidly expanding industrial city at home.

It was probably this holiday that gave him the idea of founding Princes Park, so he set about purchasing the land from Lord Sefton for £50,000 and then offered a further £10,000 to anyone who would take over the park and run it, hoping that the City would take up the offer. Unfortunately, nobody was interested so he decided that he had to shoulder the entire burden himself, which financially crippled him.

City parks were an innovation at the time, Birkenhead's being one of the first in Britain and it was the designer of that park, Sir.Joseph Paxton, whom Yates engaged, along with a Mr.Pennethorne, to lay out his new park and gardens. Ultimately, in 1849, Yates donated the Park to the City that he loved.

It was on Sunday, 30th.Nov.1856 that Yates died, his body being buried in the family vault at the Ancient Chapel, Park Road. The funeral was unusual in that his coffin was conveyed on the shoulders of the bearers rather than be transported in a hearse, which the family would have been well able to afford.

Princes Park, still a pleasant place for a stroll, actually contains the last vestiges of the Ancient Toxteth Forest in which King John once hunted deer.

I came across the Donkey's gravestone in the park, nicely decorated with flowers that someone had recently placed in front. Judy died on 12th. August 1926, aged 26 years. She must have been well loved and quite a part of the life of the park to have been so well commemorated.

Calderstones Park

This, surely our loveliest park, was originally the home of Charles Mc.Iver, one of the founders of the Cunard Line, and was bought by the Corporation for conversion into Calderstones Park in which there are a couple of very interesting monuments.

A stone plaque can be seen commemorating the planting of the first two of a row of trees by the Lord Mayor and Lady Mayoress, Alderman and Mrs.F.T.Richardson, my grandparents, to be covered in a separate booklet available in due course.

Jet of Iada

In the Old English Garden can be seen this unusual and fascinating memorial to Jet of Iada, a black Alsatian dog which lived locally and was a hero in its lifetime.

Jet's owner, Mrs.Babcock-Cleaver, lived nearby and, as the last War dragged on, was finding it difficult enough to get food for herself, never mind her dog, Jet. She decided to send him to the Forces to be used for the duration of the War in any way in which he could be useful.

At only nine months old, he was the youngest and also one of the first dogs to arrive at the Staverton Court War-dog Training School at Cheltenham. On arrival, he received his "kit" just like any other new recruit, but his included a food-bowl, brush, comb, dress collar and training collar!

After only a month's training, Jet passed out as a fully fledged guard dog and was sent to Northern Ireland to work with the American Army Air Force,

Fig.122- The Donkey's grave

together with his new handler there, Elmer Aleksiewiez, with whom he established an instant rapport.

After only a year, he was back at Staverton Court as a trainer/instructor dog, and it was during this time that Colonel Baldwin had the idea that maybe these dogs might be trained to spot snipers, a big problem to our men as they were liberating towns in enemy territory.

Colonel Baldwin's ideas were put to the test in a blitzed part of Birmingham, where several of the instructors hid in the ruins to see if they could be found by the dogs.

The exercise was a great success, the dogs soon finding all of the men, who then gathered together for a cuppa. But Jet was still scratching away at a hole in the rubble which was only about 3" across, his insistence prompting the men to dig down to see what he had found. Much to their surprise, they found one of their colleagues, who had entered an old cellar sealing himself in with just this small hole, twelve feet down, through which to breathe! Even this joker hadn't been able to outwit Jet, who became the hero of the day!

This incident gave birth to the idea that the dogs could be trained to find victims buried in the rubble after the air raids, and this became Jet's next job, one in which he never failed. One particular incident really made his name, earning him the Dickin Medal, the canine VC, he being one of the first dogs to receive such an honour.

Fig.123- Jet of Iada monument

A Chelsea hotel had been left in ruins by a really bad air raid, only one tall building left standing. The rescuers were finally satisfied that all of the bodies had been recovered from the rubble but Jet wouldn't leave, standing still and pointing up at the only wall still left upright, high against the sky. Nobody could be up there, they said, but Jet's handler, Sgt. Wardle, said Jet never makes a mistake, and so convincing was he in belief of his partner, that the others toiled with ladders and lights for 11½ hours, eventually finding a 63 year-old woman on the second floor level of that wall, entombed in fallen plaster! Only two weeks later, she was out of hospital and back into her usual routine! This wasn't the only time that Jet and his partner dog, Thorn, had found survivors when all the others had given up.

At the end of the War, Jet collected funds for the PDSA, People's Dispensary for Sick Animals, and it was common for ecstatic survivors to recognise their saviour and rush across the street, throw their arms around him in tears, and empty their purses into his collecting tin. With the flying bombs crashing around him, Jet had saved over fifty such lucky people!

By special invitation, Jet took part in the 1946 London Victory Parade, leading the Civil Defence section, during this period in his life spending most of his time at the Tower of London, collecting for the PDSA.

In December 1946, Jet was finally de-mobbed, returning home to a quiet life, punctuated only by guest appearances at fetes and parades, the excitement of which Jet enjoyed to the full.

A mining disaster in August 1947 at William Pit, Whitehaven, brought a request for Jet's help in locating bodies lost in the mine. His owner wasn't keen at all, thinking that Jet had done enough and deserved his retirement. But, having been brought up in a mining area, her mind flashed back to memories of anguished days of disasters, wailing hooters and weeping wives, so she decided to let Jet go and help.

When Jet saw the van arrive, he was playing in the garden and suddenly looked sad, as if he was being sent away again from the home that he loved. All the way, he lay there, lifeless but, as they neared Whitehaven, he reared up, "smelling" disaster and realising that he was needed once again.

Two other dogs had been brought from Staverton Court and, under Jet's leadership, they found all of the bodies. Jet had never been underground before, but he took it all in his stride. At one point, however, Jet froze then suddenly lunged away from the proposed route straight ahead. His handler took his advice, and the whole rescue party was narrowly saved just before the roof fell in! For this service, Jet was awarded the RSPCA's Medallion for Valour, presented to him by the Lord Mayor at the Town Hall.

Jet now settled into his well-deserved and quiet retirement, but he developed an illness that so weakened him that one day he couldn't even lift his ball to go and play in the garden. He settled down in his basket, took a last loving look at his mistress and died, only seven years old, but a hero just the same.

Jet lies at peace, beneath the monument erected in his honour.

Harthill

The interesting figures, see overleaf, are to be seen at the entrance to Calderstones Park on Calderstones Road, this part of the park once being the estate of John Bibby, whose mansion has now gone.

On the site of Barclay's Bank in Water Street once stood Brown's Buildings, designed by J.A.Picton and owned by William Brown, and these figures, formerly part of that building, were moved here on its demolition. The two caryatids, known as Gog and Magog, used to frame the Water Street entrance, the other figures, the Four Seasons, stood high up on the facade. Spring seems to have lost her right hand but must have been sowing seed from her basket. Summer looks like she is feeling the heat as she collects her flowers. Autumn has gathered in some wheat, while old lady Winter looks quite grim.

Fig. 124- Spring

Fig. 126- Autumn

Fig. 125- Summer

Fig. 127- Winter

Fig.128- A caryatid, Magog

Gateacre Village

After West Derby, Gateacre could be said to be the most interesting Village within the City and is well worth a visit, preferably on one of the Merseyguide walks which are most illuminating. Gateacre, despite all the new property surrounding it, retains much of interest even today.

The bust of Queen Victoria frowns beneath the trees, the base stating that "This Monument and Village Green were presented as a memorial of the Jubilee of Victoria, Queen of Great Britain and Ireland, Empress of India, by Sir.Andrew Barclay Walker Bart., High Sheriff of Lancashire 1886-87". The bust was made by Count Gleichen and was presented to Gateacre on 24th.May 1887. Sir.Andrew is very much entwined with the story of Gateacre and I recommend Derek Whale's Lost Villages of Liverpool for the whole story. He was the man, of Walker's Ales fame, who donated the Walker Art Gallery, despite opposition from the Temperance lobbies. The bust, after an initial and elaborate restoration, is now ceremoniously washed and waxed in what has now become a yearly ritual by the local children, an excellent custom that could readily be extended to many public monuments, generating a local pride in the environment that is somewhat lacking these days.

On one side of the Green is a tree planted in 1953 by the children of Gateacre to commemorate the Coronation of Queen Elizabeth II, and a further plaque tells us that the Green was restored on the occasion of the Queen's Silver Jubilee in June 1977.

Near to the aforementioned tree stands a lovely little stone gazebo, once containing a fountain. In its walls are intricately carved some animals, twin-tailed mermaids with cymbals and horns and a Liver bird. An enormous gargoyle leaps out of one side (not shown).

The inscription reads "Erected by the People of Gateacre in Memory of John H.Wilson 1883." Councillor John Hays Wilson lived at Lee Hall on what is now Lee Park Golf Club, his connection with water being that he was Chairman of the Liverpool Water Committee at the time when the great plans were being drawn up to construct Lake Vyrnwy to supply us with Welsh water, which, incidentally, it has never failed to do, even in times of drought.

Wilson opened up the grounds and gorgeous gardens of his house to the public, and even organised the Tarbock Races in the same grounds from 1881. Unfortunately, at the first race meeting, he caught a cold, from the effects of which he died in that year.

Fig.129- Queen Victoria

Fig.130- Gateacre Village, The Fountain

Fig.131- Fountain, detail

Fig.132- Fountain, weird animal

Fig.133- Fountain, detail

Fig.134- Fountain, detail

Mossley Hill

This fountain (see overleaf) can be seen, set into the perimeter wall, outside Mossley Hill Church in Elmswood Road.

To celebrate the centenary of the church in 1975, a booklet was produced by Mr.E.H.Smith which gives a history of the church and a description. Although all of the windows were lost in the War, plaques naming the donors remain and one tells us that the window, now lost, and the drinking fountain outside, were presented by John & Mary Temple, late in the 19th. Century.

John Temple, latterly of Mossley Bank, Elmswood Road, Aigburth, was born in Colne, Lancashire, on 18th.April 1839. His father, Robert, was a banker in Colne and gave John a private education following which he entered the Telegraph Service about 1852, joining the Atlantic Telegraph Company on its foundation in 1856, helping to lay the first trans-Atlantic cable from the Agamemnon.

Fig.135- Mossley Hill, the Fountain

It appears that he married in 1867, both he and his wife, Mary, being enthusiastically involved in the Church and the People's Hall. During World War One, John was involved in work for the Admiralty, for which he was awarded the honour of Commander of the Bath on 2nd.Jan.1917. Sadly, his joy was to be marred by the death of his wife in June of the same year, the funeral arrangements being handled by Messrs. George Henry Lee.

John Temple C.B. died on 17th.May 1922 in Llangamarch, South Wales, aged 83, having led a full and meaningful life, giving his heart and support to his adopted city of Liverpool.

Sefton Park

The full story of Sefton Park can be learned from the Sefton Park Civic Society's excellent book on the area. Interestingly, the Park was once part of King John's deer park and one of his lodges still exists, although altered, after 777 years!

The land for the park was bought from Lord Sefton for £263,000 but £146,000 more was needed to turn it into the park that we see today, work starting in 1867. Bearing in mind that the city was in a depressed state at the time, the American Civil War having dealt local trade a savage blow, it can be seen that this could be deemed to be expenditure on a colossal scale.

Twenty-nine entries were submitted for the design of the new park, the winner being Eduard André, Gardener in Chief to the City of Paris. Although granted the prize of £300, his designs were considered a little too lavish so a Lewis Hornblower was appointed as André's assistant, possibly to guard against excessive expenditure of the Ratepayers' cash! The Park was eventually opened by Prince Arthur of Connaught on Whit Monday, 1872.

Unfortunately, the park has been the scene of a series of extremely determined art thefts, involving the organised removal of statues and plaques of great artistic merit. Therefore some of these illustrations are now of historical interest.

After more cable work in Malta, John returned to England to help in the laying of the second Atlantic cable from the Great Eastern in 1865-6. It was after these adventurous episodes in his life that he settled in Liverpool, becoming involved with the Warrington Wire Rope Works and investing in the Durham coalfields.

He eventually became Chairman of the Wire Rope Works but always had the lives of the ordinary people at heart. In 1899 he donated a People's Hall in Aigburth in which the ordinary folk could amuse themselves and meet each other without having to go to ale-houses.

Fig.136- Fountain, detail inside

Fig.137- Sefton Park Palmhouse

51

Palm House

The wonderful Palm House, a cosy retreat on a winter's day, was built by Mackenzie and Moncur of Edinburgh. It cost between ten and twelve thousand pounds and was the gift of Henry Yates Thompson, grand nephew of Richard Vaughan Yates, the founder of Princes Park and a member of one of the City's oldest families. Born in 1838, he trained in law, but never practised, preferring politics as a career. His vast fortune of nearly £2 million is said to have come from the estate of his late father. He was especially generous to his home town, also donating the Stanley Park Conservatory.

The Palm House was opened on 5th.Oct.1896 by Alderman Joseph Ball, Chairman of the Parks, Gardens and Improvement Committee in the presence of Mr.& Mrs. Yates Thompson and the Lord Mayor, who presented Mr.Ball with a gold key as a token of the opening ceremony.

Unfortunately, a bomb which dropped nearby in the May 1941 blitz broke all of the glass, the naked shell of the building having to wait until 1950 to be re-glazed, costing half of what the whole place had originally cost to build!

Inside could once be seen a lovely collection of sculpture but, in 1986, two of the pieces were stolen by very determined thieves. The girl in the bath, by P.Park of London in 1840, was lost but was discovered for sale in Sotheby's a year or so later. Flora was stolen, only to be found in a back yard in

Fig.139- Flora, Goddess of Spring

Fig.138- Child in the bath

Fig.140- Highland Mary

Tue Brook. Unfortunately, not long after her return to the Palm House, she was stolen once again but never recovered. Highland Mary is by Benjamin E.Spence and the inscription reads "The golden hours on angel wings, flew o'er me and my dearie, for dear to me as light and life, was my sweet Highland Mary" She was the girl that Robert Burns loved more than any other, but, unfortunately, she died young. Around the outside of the Palm House are to be found eight statues by L.Chavillaud, some in bronze, some in stone, depicting various explorers and naturalists of note.

Fig.141- Mother and Child

Fig.142- The Goats

Linnaeus

LINNAEUS Born in 1707 at Rashult in South Sweden, his name was then Carl Linné. His father, a Lutheran clergyman, urged the boy to study languages, including Latin, to prepare himself for a life in the Church. But Carl loved flowers rather than Latin, spending many hours collecting and studying plants, much to the detriment of his school work.

His father then took him away from school and apprenticed him to a shoe-maker but, one time when he was ill, Carl met a doctor who admired his interest in nature, sending him to live with a colleague of his. The colleague encouraged young Carl, eventually getting him into Uppsala University where he was to meet Olaf Celsius, the naturalist. It was in Olaf's home that Carl worked out his theory of classification of plants based on the variations of their sex organs.

Fig.143- Carl Linnaeus

After considerable hard work, Carl was commissioned by the Stockholm Academy of Sciences to carry on his research in Lapland. He set out in 1732, eventually covering 4,000 miles on his journeys which took him to Denmark, Hamburg and Holland where he stayed for three years. While in Holland he met a Banker called Clifford who, in 1736, sent Carl to England. In 1737 he published his Lapland findings, following which he returned to Uppsala to take up the post of Professor of Medicine & Botany, a position which he was to hold for 36 years during which time the King of Sweden made him Royal Physician and a Noble.

It was then, in 1761, that he called himself Carl Von Linné. Strangely for one who loathed his early Latin studies, it was that language in which his books were printed, Latin being then the universal language as is English today. His name in Latin appeared as Linnaeus, the name by which he is remembered for all time. He stayed at Uppsala until his death in 1778.

In the early days of Botany, classification of plants was rather chaotic, involving folklore, superstition and vague descriptions. Plants with medicinal properties were much sought-after and when world travel became more general, it was realised that a better method had to be found in which to classify all the new plants then being brought back from distant lands.

Originally, all plants with grass-like leaves would be in one group, those with bulbous swellings in another and so on. It was Linnaeus who, in 1735, established twenty-four classes of plants, based on the characters of their sex organs. He also introduced the system of naming plants using two words, called the Binomial System. One name is the type, the other the variation of that type.

Charles Darwin

Born in Shrewsbury in 1809, Darwin died in 1882 and is buried in Westminster Abbey.

Darwin travelled widely, collecting plant specimens, in 1858 devising his theory of Natural Selection, whereby the strongest will survive, each generation being slightly stronger than the last. In time, he suggested, a new species of plant would appear that bore no resemblance to its distant ancestor.

Darwin submitted his theory to the Linnaean Society in 1858 followed by his Origin of the Species in 1859 but outraged the Church by offending the feelings of the time by not linking his theory to The Creation. W.E.H.Lecky at the time said that the success of any opinion depends much less upon the force of its arguments, or upon the ability of its advocates, than upon the predisposition of Society to receive it. Good advice!

Captain Cook

Volumes have been written about Captain James Cook, the great naval explorer, but a brief story is all that is required here.

He was born on 27th.Oct.1728 at Marton in Cleveland, Yorkshire, the family moving, in 1736, to Great Ayton, five miles away. It was there that James went to school and, in 1746, after four years on the family farm, took his first sea journey on the collier Freelove.

Fig.145- Captain James Cook

On 17th.June 1755 he joined the Royal Navy, working his way up until, on his 29th birthday in 1757, he was appointed Master of HMS Pembroke.

His first voyages were to Canada surveying the St.Lawrence, during which he was involved in the capture of Quebec. He married during this period and, by 1768, was off to the South Seas, stopping at Tahiti. The following year, he discovered and charted New Zealand and the east coast of Australia. 1772 saw him home to see his family,

Fig.144- Charles Darwin

then off in HMS Resolution to find the Southern Continent. He was the first to cross the Antarctic Circle and, in 1774, after surveying Tahiti and New Zealand, he travelled further south than anyone before, a record that was to last for 50 years.

By 1775 he was home again, but next year he was off on his final voyage, again in the Resolution. Discovering islands in the South Pacific, he then explored the north west coast of America, returning to Hawaii where he was unfortunately killed by natives.

He was a great man who cared for his men. It was Cook who found how to prevent the sailor's curse of Scurvy, caused by lack of Vitamin C, by feeding fruit to his men. A previous ship at Tahiti had 100 cases of Scurvy on board, Cook had none!

In 1934, the cottage in Great Ayton was bought and shipped, stone by stone, to Melbourne, Australia, where it now stands in Fitzroy Gardens in surroundings that could easily be deepest England. The shipping line performed this service free of charge and even the creeper on the wall was transported! When I visited the cottage, I found it a lovely tribute to the discoverer of Australia and lovingly maintained. In return, Melbourne sent an obelisk of stone quarried from near the spot where Cook first set foot in Australia and this was to be erected in Great Ayton.

At the time of writing, the statue had been taken away for safe keeping by the Council.

André le Notre

Fig. 146- André Notre

Born in Paris in 1613, Le Notre lived there until his death in 1700. He was the first person in history to call himself a Landscape Architect. It was he who designed the fabulous gardens at Versailles for Louis XIV, and London's St.James's Park. I saw the gardens at Versailles in pouring rain and yet they still looked good, surely a tribute to Le Notre's skills!

Prince Henry the Navigator

Fig. 147- Prince Henry the Navigator

The Portuguese were the first European nation to start exploring the seas in search of wealth. In 1415, a force, which included Prince Henry, son of King John the First, captured Ceuta in Morocco and it was from this time that Prince Henry became known as "The Navigator."

Using Ceuta as a base, Henry's ships ventured out into the unknown. By 1433, they passed Cape Bojador on the Spanish Sahara Coast and colonised Madeira and the Azores, the ships returning loaded with gold and slaves. Portugal grew rich and, although Prince Henry died soon afterwards, his lead was taken up, exploration continuing all over the world.

Such is the reverence still felt toward Prince Henry that, as recently as 1960, a staggeringly impressive monument 180ft. high and laden with the most lifelike groups of figures, all carved in stone, was erected in Lisbon beside the river near the spot from which the original ships of discovery set out. Once again, I had to admire this wonderful sight in the rain, but it was most impressive!

At the time of writing, the statue was in storage to prevent its theft.

Columbus

Fig. 148- Christopher Columbus

Appropriately engraved, this statue states that "The Discoverer of America was the Maker of Liverpool." He was also said to have doubled the size of the world by his discoveries.

Christopher Columbus was born in Genoa, Italy, son of a woolcomber. After a spell in the weaving trade, his lust for adventure took him off to sea, to the Mediterranean and England. On his return to Lisbon, he married and had a son, Diego.

Life ashore bored him, so off he went to the Equator in 1481, making measurements that convinced him, against current thought, that the world was round. His ideas were sceptically received in official Portuguese circles, so a disheartened and now widowed Columbus took his son off to Spain to try to interest the King in his theory, knowing that the Monarch was seeking a new route to the East.

By 1485, Columbus had reached a monastery at La Rabida, where the monks enthused over his ideas, seeing the discovery of new lands as a chance to enrich the Country and spread the Faith at the same time. Through the Monks' good connections, Columbus was introduced to a nobleman in Seville, who eventually had the plan presented to King Ferdinand who, only after prompting by Queen Isabella, fitted out a fleet of ships, partly paid for, it is said, by the sale of the Queen's jewels.

Power, Title and Governorship of all discovered lands was half heartedly promised to Columbus by the King, who sent him off in command of the "Santa Maria" on 3rd.Aug.1492. Following a provisioning stop at the Canary Isles, Columbus set off, on 6th.Sept., into the great unknown.

The men became more and more uneasy as the days went by, a situation that had happened before when the King of Portugal had sent out a similar mission after hearing of Columbus's story, only to have it return due to the fear of the sailors, out in the great lonely ocean. We find it hard to appreciate, in our mapped and charted world, what a great leader would be required to drive frightened and superstitious men into the unknown for 36 days. On the next day, they finally sighted land, Columbus being the first to set foot on it, Spanish flag in hand, on 12th.October.

It was the islands of Cuba, Haiti and others that Columbus was discovering and claiming for Spain, leaving a garrison there to return to Spain on 15th.March of the following year to a hero's welcome and to receive the honours promised to him by the King on his departure.

Later that year, Columbus set off again with seventeen ships and 1500 men, to discover that his garrison had been killed by the natives. Undaunted, he set up another settlement called Isabella, and spent the next two years exploring the area before returning home to report to the King.

Two years after that, he set off on a two-year voyage to the Venezuelan coast and the Orinoco River, just managing to struggle back to his settlement in the land that he had called Hispaniola, only to find that disputes had broken out, resulting in the people sending for a new Governor, who arrived to take up the post which had been officially given to Columbus by the King, right from the start.

It all ended with poor old Columbus being sent back to Spain in chains, the whole affair then being glossed over by the Royalty and, although Columbus was released, never again was he to be highly favoured by the Rulers. After the death of Isabella, Columbus's true friend at Court, the King sent him out with four leaky ships for his final voyage, from which he returned a sick and tired man to a miserable homecoming and no more money from the King.

Four years later, on 20th.May 1506, he died at Valladolid, his body being taken to the Santa Domingo Cathedral in his Hispaniola, where it lay until 1796 when it was taken to Havana Cathedral, resting there until 1899, when it was returned to Spain where it is now to be found. It is said that he asked to be buried with the chains that shackled him on that humiliating journey back to Spain from the New World. He had actually kept the chains as a macabre souvenir, perhaps to remind himself of the quirks of human nature whereby a man who has made his adopted country rich is himself treated shabbily. How many times has this happened in history?

Columbus could have been the first man to introduce rubber to Europe when he brought back bouncing balls, with which the natives played. It took the English scientist, Joseph Priestly, to find a use for this curiosity in 1770, using it to erase pencil mistakes by rubbing them out, in so doing naming the substance rubber.

At least, in Liverpool, Columbus is still remembered on Columbus Day, 12th.October, when a wreath is laid at the statue to the accompaniment of U.S. Soldiers from Burtonwood.

This is the only place in Britain that this American day is celebrated and this is believed to be the only statue of Columbus in the Country. So valuable is the figure that it now has to be kept locked away to prevent its loss to thieves.

John Parkinson

Fig.149- John Parkinson

John Parkinson, 1567-1650, was Apothecary to King James I, but is mainly known for his wonderful book of 1629 called "Paradisi in Sole, or a Garden of all sorts of Pleasant Flowers which our English air will permit to be nursed up." The Picton Library has a copy of this extremely rare book which shows what can be grown in the open and describes the appearance and medical uses of the plants. There are also line drawings, surely an innovation in 1629, when the pages are almost 8" x 10". The Flower Garden, Herb Garden and Orchard are covered with advice on how to lay them out and useful information about soil and watering.

In the Orchard section are listed 78 types of apple that were grown in those days, including the Pomewater, Marligo, Gruntlin, Cowsnout and Woman's Breast Apple! The latter was decribed as "a great apple!" At the back of the book is an index of the virtues and properties of the plants including "good for bees", "for cold and windy stomachs" and "to make excellent ink."

Strange as this may seem to our pill popping age of bottled medicines, the medicinal properties of plants were taught in medical schools until fairly recently, especially in the training for Pharmacy.

Mercator

Mercator, son of a poor shoemaker, was born on 5th.March 1512 at Rupelmonde in Flanders. He studied at Louvain and later lectured in Astronomy and Geography, making all his instruments with his own hands. He held liberal views, a dangerous thing in those days, once being one of 43 people arrested for this reason but, in 1544, he escaped leaving the others to be burnt alive. Eventually he was employed by the Emperor, for whom he made globes of wood or crystal.

It was Mercator who invented the method of drawing the map of the world divided by lines of latitude and longitude crossing each other at right-angles, a method still used today, the only disadvantage being that the Polar areas are stretched out as wide as the Equator, so accurate measurements are difficult. Mollweide improved on this by showing the world like a tennis ball cut open and flattened out, accurate, but not as easy as Mercator's maps when planning your world tour!

Mercator's first World Map was published in 1569 and he lived to a ripe old age, dying at Duisburg on 2nd.Dec. 1594.

The statue was removed by the Council for safe keeping in 1988.

Fig.150- Mercator

Peter Pan

Eros Fountain

Fig.152- Eros Fountain

Fig.151- Peter Pan

We all know the saying anything you can do, I can do better and in this case it's true! While London has its Peter Pan and Eros statues, so does Liverpool!

The installation of the Peter Pan statue, a replica of the one in London's Kensington Gardens, was celebrated by a pageant on 16th.June 1928, but it was in 1927 that Mr.George Audley, of Lulworth Road, Birkdale, presented the figure to the park. Two years later he also donated the Children's Garden containing a floral cuckoo clock and other delights, an event celebrated in Stanley Park on 21st.Sept. of that year by a "Pageant of Cuckooland" with 1200 children taking part.

Mr.Audley, a good man if ever there was one, even repeated the Pageant at the Hippodrome Theatre for the enjoyment of 2,400 poor children on Nov.2nd. of the same year.

Miss Margaret Beavan, first Lady Lord Mayor of Liverpool, formally opened the Children's Corner, in which the Peter Pan is situated, in 1931. The figure is by George Frampton. Unfortunately, in recent years, two of the delicately detailed heads have been sawn off the sculpture.

George Audley was a bachelor who loved his City, showering gifts upon it. His suitably ultimate deed was to present us with Eros, a replica of that in London. It was erected in 1932, just in time for Audley to see it before he died in Feb.1932. The fountain in London was designed by Alfred Gilbert and ours was made by the Foundry of A.B.Burton. Detailed examination is in order to discover the exquisite detail to be found around the base.

When the sculpture was officially inaugurated on 23rd.July 1932, a brass band was on hand to entertain the enthusiastic crowd which included the Lord Mayor, Alderman J.C.Cross. The fountain was even guarded by a cannon reputed to have come from the Royal Yacht.

But who exactly was Eros? We all know the name, but let us find out more about him. Eros is the Greek name for the character known as Cupid to the Romans. Cupid was the son of Aphrodite, the Goddess of Beauty and Love. He spent his time shooting golden arrows at those whom he decided should fall in love with each other, an effect which was immediate once the arrow had pierced the recipient. Occasionally, though, Cupid would get his arrows mixed up, firing one tipped with lead. This would have the opposite effect, causing hatred between those unlucky enough to receive this treatment. Many a marital strife was blamed on Cupid who was accused of being blind and was even shown blindfolded in some representations of him.

According to one story, Cupid even indirectly caused the berries of the Mulberry trees to be red rather than their original colour of white! One day Cupid was flying around, looking for likely couples for him to link in love. His travels took him to Babylonia where he spotted the noble youth, Pyramus, who lived next door to a girl called Thisbe.

Eros, thinking that he had found a well-matched couple, shot down a couple of golden arrows, then flew off to do his good deeds elsewhere, not realising that these two neighbouring families were bitter enemies and the two young lovers, who now yearned for each other were, of course, forbidden to meet.

Their misery of separation was relieved one day when a shaft of sunlight, shining at an unusual angle, indicated a crack in the dividing wall between their two homes, through which the two lovers could now whisper their tender thoughts.

Determined to run away together, they arranged to slip out one night and meet under a certain white Mulberry bush that they both knew. Dusk was to be the meeting time, so Thisbe left early, wrapping a scarf around her face lest she be recognised. But, on arrival at the bush, she found herself alone so she sat down, waiting for her intended.

As she sat there quietly, the calm was suddenly broken by the roar of a lion, jumping out of the undergrowth to kill a passing ox. Although the lion wasn't actually threatening Thisbe, she fled into the woods, dropping her scarf, which the lion chewed in its inquisitive way, spitting it out, tattered and stained with ox blood.

Of course, Pyramus arrived just too late to see what had happened and, finding the bloodstained scarf which he recognised as Thisbe's, he thought the worst and immediately blamed himself for her apparent death.

True to the traditions of mythology, he decided to "do himself in," and decided to die at the place where he should have met his true love.

Out came his sword, and on it he threw himself, sinking to the ground to spend his last moments thinking of his lover as he faded away. Thisbe, meanwhile, ventured out from the safety of the cave where she had been hiding and decided to see if the coast was clear, only to discover the terrible sight of her man, lying there dead.

With nothing left to live for, she decided to join him, if only in death. Pausing only to kiss Pyramus, she too fell on his sword, the two of them to be found lying together by their parents the following morning.

Realising that there must have been a bond between the two young people, the parents had them buried together. But the Mulberry tree had absorbed the blood that had flowed beneath its roots and, forever after, the bush and all its successors have borne red berries!

Actually, Cupid himself eventually got married to a girl called Psyche who didn't realise that she had married a god, because Cupid appeared to her in disguise, and only at night when she could not see him.

He set up his wife in an enchanted palace, coming to her each night through the window. One night, Psyche decided that she would have a look at this husband of hers, to see if he was ugly as her

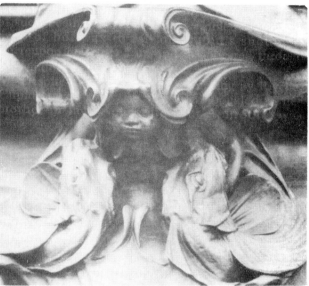

Fig. 153-5- Eros Fountain, details

teasing sisters had suggested. Candle in hand, she crept into the darkened bedroom to discover a man of such beauty that her hand trembled, causing a drop of hot wax to fall on Cupid's shoulder, whereupon he jumped up and disappeared through the window in an instant.

Despite desperate nights of weeping by Psyche, Cupid stayed away, so she then appealed to her mother in law, Aphrodite. But Aphrodite was furious at Psyche's behaviour, designating various difficult tasks for her to perform in order that she could buy herself back into favour with the gods.

The first mammoth task, of sorting millions of seeds and grain into separate piles, was eased by the help of a friendly and sympathetic army of ants, but the next task she had to perform on her own.

This ordeal took her into the bowels of the earth, to Hades itself, to obtain a jar of special ointment which would help the Goddess Aphrodite remain as beautiful as ever. Having braved the terrors of the "lower world", Psyche wondered what it was for which she had suffered so much in order to obtain. So she opened the jar, but the influence of what was within sent her into a deep sleep; the sleep, of course, was considered to be the greatest aid to beauty.

There would have been no awakening for Psyche, had not her husband, Cupid, come along and taken pity on his erring wife. Swooping down on his little wings, he awakened her with a kiss, and they lived happily ever after!

Samuel Smith

Born in Kirkcudbrightshire on 4th.Jan.1836, Samuel Smith entered a family engaged in farming on the grand scale. His grandfather being a Presbyterian Minister probably prompted Samuel's father to send the lad off to Edinburgh University to study for the Ministry. It was during this time that it came to light that he possessed considerable intellectual powers and that he was also a great believer in doing good for mankind.

Notwithstanding his religious beliefs, Samuel decided to make his career in commerce and left for Liverpool to join the cotton-broking firm of Logan & Co., attending the Presbyterian Church in Canning Street in his spare time.

He soon became very popular at Logan's, owing to his peculiarly keen sense of sight and touch by which, in a remarkably short time, he became a well renowned expert at judging the quality of cotton. In fact, long before the end of his apprenticeship, he was considered to be more of an asset to the firm than those members who had been there for many years!

Determined to make his fortune, he realised that education was the first step, so off he set on a twelve months tour of the USA to learn the other side of the cotton industry and to make connections which would, hopefully, be of use to him in the future. A good writer, he sent back many letters to the Liverpool Daily Post, describing his exploits and the various aspects of the cotton industry.

Unfortunately, just as he was starting home, the American Civil War was beginning, bringing with it the threat of disruption to cotton supplies and the subsequent industrial and economic chaos in the Lancashire mill towns. The Manchester Chamber of Commerce, who had by now heard of Smith, implored him to tour India and the Far East to try to organise alternate supplies from there. Following his favourable report, the Indian plantations were improved and supplies of cotton began to reach us from there.

Fig.156- Samuel Smith Obelisk

In 1860 he finally opened up his own office at 4,Chapel Street. Apart from his matchless knowledge of cotton, Smith's incredible skill as a financier and speculator soon earned him enormous wealth. In 1864, he married Melville, daughter of the Rev.Dr.Christison of Biggar. She was to live until 1893, during which time she enthusiastically helped her husband in every aspect of his life's works.

Smith's income was matched only by his generosity, always mindful of his religious upbringing. He was a big financial supporter of the YMCA and helped to establish what is now the NSPCC, but the exact extent of his philanthropy has never been determined.

His political career began by his being elected to the Council in 1878 representing the Castle Street ward, being re-elected in 1882, his favourite subjects for involvement being those concerning the social and health issues.

Dec.1882 saw him elected to Parliament as a Liberal, much to the surprise of the ruling Tory Party of the City. What had helped his success against his oponent, Mr.A.B.Forwood, was the extent of his generosity which, knowing no bounds of creed, had included Catholics who had been encouraged by their Priests at Mass to vote for him. More votes were gained through his oratory and the content of his election literature. In a total vote of 36,087 votes cast, he won with a majority of 309!

Fig.157- Samuel Smith

Fig.158- Samuel Smith Obelisk, Virtue, Evil and Youth

Following the reorganisation of the ward boundaries, he lost his seat in 1885, deciding to use his newly found leisure to visit India so that he could renew his contacts there. While away, he was elected in his absence as MP for Flintshire, a seat that he held until his death on 28th.Dec.1906 in Calcutta.

Strangely, for a man that apparently had everything, he died alone and lonely. His wife had died in 1893 after nearly thirty years of happy marriage, and his son, Gordon, to whom he was devoted, died of Typhoid in 1898, aged only 28.

The monument, by Charles J.Allen, was erected by public subscription and was unveiled by the Lord Mayor on 21st.May 1909. It is 60ft. high and of red granite, the architectural details being designed by Willink & Thicknesse.

An inscription reads "Whosoever drinketh of this water shall thirst again, but whosoever drinketh of the water that I shall give him shall never thirst." The panels, designed and modelled by C.J.Allen and cast by A.B.Burton of Thames Ditton, showed Samuel Smith, Virtue Thrusting Evil from the path of Youth and Indian Famine Relief but have all been stolen since these pictures were taken in 1987.

Samuel Smith founded various missions around the city, one of which only closed in 1977. He helped Dr.Barnardo in his struggles for the orphaned children of London, a truly great man.

Fig.159- Samuel Smith Obelisk, Indian Famine Relief

Rathbone the Fifth

The Rathbone family is punctuated by a long line of William Rathbones, No.5 being commemorated in Sefton Park, and No.6 in St.Johns Gardens.

The family were sawyers in the 18th. century but, by 1730, were noted as being shipbuilders and shipowners, ships then, of course, being made of wood. Traditionally a family of Quakers, they became involved in the cotton trade when William Rathbone No.4 imported the first cotton from the USA into this country in 1798, a commodity that was to become their greatest business interest.

William Rathbone 5th. was born in Liverpool on 17th.June 1787 and after initial schooling at Hackney, was educated at Oxford by his tutor, Theophilus Houlbroke. In later life he was known as an eminent educationalist and philanthropist and was an advocate of Roman Catholic emancipation and Parliamentary and Municipal reform." His father had disagreed with the Quakers' policy of expulsion of members involved in mixed marriages, and Rathbone 5th. was so expelled after his

Fig.160- William Rathbone V statue

marriage in 1812 to Elizabeth Greg of Quarry Bank, Styal.

He finally left the Friends in 1829 and had a long and happy marriage, Elizabeth living until she was 93! He was a lover of art, but also a serious politician. In 1831 he introduced polling booths, fought against corruption in politics and was one of the very few men in Liverpool at that time to back the anti-slavery campaign. He was Mayor in 1837.

He died on 1st.Feb.1868 and is commemorated by this wonderful statue overlooking the lake in Sefton Park, which was unveiled on 1st.Jan.1877 by Mr.James Aikin.

The beautiful panels, by T.Brock, were executed in 1876 and showed Education, Feeding the Poor and Importing the Cotton. They were all stolen in 1987. The faces on the figures were exquisite.

Fig.162- William Rathbone V statue, Feeding the Poor

Fig.161- William Rathbone V statue, Education

Fig.163- William Rathbone V statue, Importing the bales of cotton

Stanley Park

Fig.164- Stanley Park

Palmhouse

Stanley Park was laid out in the years 1867-70 by Edward Kemp, opened by the Mayor on 14th.May 1870 and is now in a rather sad state. At the time, the Corporation paid £117,500 for the land on which to make this park, the cost of so doing adding a further £50,000 to the bill. In those days the park boasted a 300 yard long terrace which was fitted out with iron stands on which the gentlemen could rest their telescopes to get a steady view of, presumably, their ships arriving in the Mersey or could it be that rather nice lady who lives in the villa down the road?

The Palm House, originally known as the Gladstone Conservatory, was designed and erected by Mackenzie & Moncur of Edinburgh, London & Glasgow in 1899. It was donated by Henry Yates Thompson, cost £8,000 and was presented by him to the City on 23rd.April 1900.

In July 1986, the Council sold off many unwanted buildings including this Palm House which had been abandoned by them and subsequently seriously vandalised. A Rodney Street company was reported to have paid £15,000 for the building which was to require £40,000 more in repairs under the guidance of their architect. The building has been tastefully converted into a licenced restaurant, and is well worth a visit.

The Palm House once housed a lifesize marble statue of Flora Macdonald but, shortly after these pictures were taken, with Council permission, the figure was almost totally wrecked.

The statue was by Benjamin E.Spence and was donated by George Audley in Jan.1929. It was Mr Audley who provided the Peter Pan and Eros figures in Sefton Park. In the photographs, the beautiful proportions of the figure can be seen, even down to the thistle at her feet.

Flora Macdonald lived from 1722 to 1790 and, when she was 23, she took the fugitive Bonnie Prince Charlie to the Isle of Skye in a boat, the

Fig.165- Stanley Park, Flora Macdonald

Prince dressed as a servant girl called Betty Burke. The only daughter of Ranald Macdonald of Milton, Flora was arrested on 12th.July 1746, only eleven days after leaving the Prince at the Inn of Portree.

Taken to the Tower of London, she was released the following year and returned home to marry Allan Macdonald of Armadale. They emigrated to America in 1774 where they were caught up in the

Fig.166- Stanley Park, Flora Macdonald

of wounds, some of disease, all in the devoted performance of duty".

The faint traces can still be seen, on the sides of the cross, of the names of the men concerned. The Memorial itself has been around a bit because, according to the inscriptions on the other three sides, it started life in Portsmouth in 1863, "Removed to Chelsea in 1877", then "Removed to Liverpool in 1911".

To determine the story behind the monument, we must know just a little general history of the British involvement in India. Actually, it was the Portuguese who established the first European colony at Goa, on the west coast of India, but their influence was weakened by their attempts at suppressing the Hindu religion.

Politics in the Mother country always affected affairs in the Colonies, and the Spanish control over Portugal in 1580 meant that Goa was neglected by its rulers. Meanwhile the English, Dutch and French began to move in, trying to get a foothold in India and get into the trade that had previously been the monopoly of the Arabs.

Wars and conflicts between the English and French at home were duplicated in India, both sides using to their own advantage the endless warring between the rulers of the mini-states of India, conquering them one by one.

So important was commerce that it was actually the East India Company that ruled British interests in India, the French operating a similar system in the parts of the country under their control.

American War of Independence in which her husband was captured at the Battle of Moores Creek. Yet, after all her adventures, she returned to Scotland in her old age to live out the last of her days in her home land.

The pendant that Flora is wearing is called a Luckenbooth, the name given to the shops that used to sell this sort of jewellery. The first such shop was in Edinburgh near St.Giles' Cathedral as far back as the 16th.Century. The design, linked hearts surmounted with a crown, is traditionally a love symbol and pendants of this type can still be bought in Scotland.

Whitley Gardens Shaw Street

These gardens were named after Edward Whitley MP, but the drinking fountain unveiled in his honour on 1st.Sept.1896 is no longer there.

The one thing of interest is this large cross, happily to say, beautifully restored in 1986, its surroundings admirably improved since the photographs were taken. The inscription on the front tells us that "This Cross commemorates the services and death of 243 Officers, N.C. Officers and Private Soldiers lost by the 8th., The Kings Regiment, while engaged in suppressing the Great Sepoy Mutiny of 1857-8. Some died in battle, some

Fig.167- The Cross in Whitley Gardens

The famous Clive of India started out as a clerk with the East India Company, but went on to become Lord Clive, protector of our interests out there. Following a treaty made in Paris in 1763, the effective withdrawal of French forces in India started, leaving the British supreme.

Even today, India presents itself as a country of strange customs and beliefs, but in those days some of the common practices appeared so bizarre that the British tried to eradicate them. These included the burning of widows and the feeding of infants to crocodiles!

It was the Hindus who most resented the interference in their traditional lifestyle, even resenting the building of the railways without which India would be lost today. Law and order was maintained by the employment of Sepoys who were Native men serving in the British Army.

At the time, the rifles in use fired cartridges which needed to be smeared with grease. Nobody was quite sure where the fat originated to make the grease, whether it came from pigs which were considered unclean by the Mohammedans, or from cows which were considered Holy by the Hindus, but the one thing that was certain was that the religious Sepoys were outraged.

In May 1857, the Sepoys began their rebellion at Meerut, killing all the Europeans, then marching to Delhi in order to do the same thing there and then put a descendant of one of the former Moguls on the Throne.

Unfortunately, the British Commander had died of Cholera and, using the situation, the rebels gained support and considerable territory following one massacre after another.

By September, the British began to repel the rebels, starting at Lucknow, but requiring until the following March to completely regain control.

The British Government realised that it was not the place of a trading company to administer a country comprising such a variety of peoples and customs. They decided that a Viceroy be appointed to rule on behalf of the Crown, Queen Victoria being crowned Empress of India in 1877.

The first Viceroy, Lord Canning, ruled with kid gloves to try to heal the wounds of bitterness, and gradually things quietened down and the history of India continued. The Kings Liverpool Regiment was involved in this action and more details of their adventures can be obtained from the Liverpool Museum where a whole gallery is dedicated to them.

The carvings on the central shaft of the cross are fairly eroded by time and weather and it is rather a guess as to what is depicted.

It is probable that we are seeing artistic impressions of the battle. The top panel appears to show men (soldiers?) encamped as it looks like a pointed army tent on the left and a tree on the right. The central panel depicts two warriors at battle, fighting across a dead man. The lower scene shows two people carrying away the wounded.

Botanic Gardens

In the Botanic Gardens in Edge Lane can be found two figures mounted on plinths, representing Tam O'Shanter and Souter Johnny. As they are in such poor condition as to be unrecognisable, they have had to be omitted.

Bootle

Overshadowed by its "Big Brother" Liverpool, Bootle no doubt prospered by the success of its neighbour in the boom years of the last century, especially as the Liverpool docks spread themselves across Bootle's waterfront, creating work, wealth and destroying what had been peaceful seaside districts.

Bootle shared in the immense profits made from shipping and industry, as can be seen by the mansions still preserved in the Merton Road area and in the magnificent public buildings that the Borough was able to erect in the Balliol Road and Oriel Road area.

One of my most prized possessions is a cast-iron Bootle lamp-post that I purchased from them for a few pounds, identical to those in Liverpool except that Bootle went the whole hog, spent that bit extra, and had their lovely coat-of-arms set into both sides of the posts with the maker's name at the bottom,

Fig. 168- Whitley Gardens Cross, detail

Brown Duncan & Co. of Bootle! How about that for civic pride?

Unfortunately, the close proximity of its mighty neighbour backfired on Bootle when it came to wartime. The concentration of docks and industry made the Borough the target for the heaviest and most destructive enemy bombing of anywhere in Britain, suffering appalling loss of life and property. Such was the extent of the damage done to the Borough in the war years that the 1939 population figure of 80,000 was reduced, by 1941, to a daytime population of 30,000 and as low as 10,000 at night. The bombing was so intense that over 2,000 houses were destroyed, and of the remaining 15,000, only 40 escaped damage altogether.

Poor old Bootle, for which I have quite an affection, has never really recovered from its battle scars, although the injection of jobs through the new office blocks has helped a lot. Of course, as Liverpool goes through its crisis of unemployment allied with the usual associated social problems, Bootle cannot break free, tending to suffer alongside its "Siamese Twin" from which it can never be parted.

Those who travel along Stanley Road and other routes which lead out of the Borough and into Liverpool may notice how the house numbers, lamp-posts and pavements all change at the boundary, proving that good old Bootle still asserts its proud independence in the face of all odds! We shall now look around at some interesting monuments in this friendly and historic place.

Mark Connolly Island

As far as I know, this traffic island, at the top of Merton Road, is the only one anywhere to bear a name plate. It has fascinated me for 25 years, since I first worked in Bootle, and this was actually the reason that the boundaries of this book were extended to include Bootle, although I have found other interesting stories about the Borough as well.

In the May elections of 1952, the Labour Party gained control of Bootle, ousting the Conservatives, and Mark Connolly, a Labour man, was appointed to the office of Mayor. A row then broke out as the Conservatives said that, following a newly-made agreement between the parties that they should alternately appoint Mayors no matter which party was in control at the time, it was their turn to field one of their men into that office. But, despite initial rumblings of discontent, Mark Connolly stayed in office for his full twelve months.

Fig.169- Mark Connolly Island, plaque

Mark was born in Bootle and brought up in Bootle Village in a family well used to hard times, something that he never forgot all his life.

By 1952, he had served on the Council for 21 years and had been an official of the Transport & General Workers' Union, a post from which he resigned on becoming Mayor. He had served the Union for 15 years, had been a Councillor for Knowsley ward from 1919-22, Mersey ward from 1926 and 1936-40 following which he was elected as Alderman..

He had served on most committees, but was particularly interested in the Works Committee. In his youth he had been a participant in a most unlikely duo of sports, bowls and American Football!

Fig.170 Mark Connolly Island, Merton Road

As Mrs.Connolly was an invalid, Mark's daughter, Maureen, was to be the youngest ever Mayoress at 23 years old. The new Mayor was installed in office on Wednesday, 21st.May 1952, the following Sunday seeing him on his first official function, leading a procession to church. He decided that they would walk from the Town Hall, up Merton Road, past his home at 73, Worcester Road and on to St.Monica's Church. This way, his house-bound wife could see him in his robes of office as he passed, surely moments of deep satisfaction for the poor lady. The non-Catholics peeled off the procession and into Christ Church in Merton Road to have their own service, re-joining the others later on.

It was a lovely sunny day and, what with the excitement and the four marching bands, it must have been a day to talk about for weeks! It was just as well it was a nice day for Mrs.Connolly to enjoy because, sadly, she died on Saturday, 9th.August of that year.

During his year of office, Mark had the joy and honour to be the first to try out the new Official Car, a gorgeous Humber limousine! It was during this year that the Scott's "Empire" bakery was opened in Dunnings Bridge Road and work started on the vast English Electric factory further down the same road, both places now closed down. The Netherton estates were about to be laid out, schools being built and great plans and hopes being put into action. It was also the year that the great ocean liner, the Empress of Britain, caught fire and capsized in the Bootle docks.

Mark's year of office was well received by all, a feat of popularity achieved with no little help from his daughter and Mayoress, Maureen, who was acclaimed by all who met her. During my research, I had the pleasure to meet Maureen, and I can see why she was such a good Mayoress. I found her most charming and helpful. Her brother, Tom, has also been of great assistance to me in rooting out facts and information regarding his father and I am most grateful to them both.

But, our story doesn't end here because, although he gave up his Union work at the start of his year of Office, Mark was still with the Council, ultimately becoming Chairman of the Works Committee.

On 3rd.April 1959, reports were published of plans to spend £70,000 on converting Merton Road into a dual carriageway to improve traffic flow, especially at the top end by Christ Church. By 17th.July, the residents had called a meeting at which they opposed the scheme, especially as it involved the loss of part of their gardens. The proposed road, they said, would only funnel the traffic down into a bottleneck further along and it was being said that the money would be better spent on the new swimming baths being considered for Netherton, but ultimately never built.

By 16th.October of that year, the dual carriageway seems to have been forgotten, but the severe problems at the junction of the five roads, Merton Road, Hawthorne Road, Oxford Road and Breeze Hill, had to be resolved. A complicated set of traffic lights at this junction was impeding the flow of the 11,000 vehicles daily crossing the junction and the church was complaining of the noise outside as well.

Work had to be started soon in order that it be completed by the following March to qualify for a grant towards the cost. Permission to start the job had been granted on 14th.Oct. and they must have started work soon after because, by 8th.Jan.1960, traffic was already passing round the partly built island.

Tom Connolly tells me that, amongst the jungle of traffic lights previously at this spot, there was a small triangular island on which there was a seat where his father, Mark, used to meet his pals at 8.00 pm on a Sunday night before going for a drink. It was said that all of the road schemes in Bootle were hatched out while sitting on that seat on Sunday evenings!

Mark died in May 1960, aged 72, having served Bootle on the Council since 1919. In those days there was no recompense for lost wages whilst attending Council meetings, although there were many times of unemployment when there were no wages for Mark to lose. Contemporary reports tell us of his many friends, most of whom attended his funeral on 2nd.May 1960 at St.Monica's. At the next Council meeting, his colleagues paid tribute to him, standing in silence to express their respect for a sadly departed friend. Although I can find no record of it, it must have been at this time that the newly-completed traffic island, built on his favourite resting place, was named after him, surely a unique honour and a homely tribute only possible in a place like Bootle.

The Bootle Times reminded its readers of Mark's love of sport, rarely missing a cup final except this year when he went to his own final. Alderman Peter Mahon probably summed up the current feelings best when he said that "Mark Connolly's memory will always be fragrant to us in Bootle".

Visitors to Bootle may have noticed Connolly House, the Elderly Persons' Home in Balliol Road. This was actually named after Mark's brother, Tom, who was Chairman of Social Services and it was he who opened Bootle's other such home, Basil Grange in West Derby.

Maureen, Mark's daughter, thinks that Connolly Avenue was named after both Mark and his brother Tom as they were both prominent men on the Council. They were big names who did well for their home town which was lucky to have had them in its midst.

Fig.171- Connolly Avenue, off Aintree Road

Fig.172- Connolly House, Balliol Road

Derby Park

Derby Park must be Bootle's oldest park, opened in 1895 in an age far removed from our own. It seems incredible that, in those days, people used to hold garden parties in its grounds!

Along the main path can be seen the drinking fountain on which is the inscription that it was "erected by subscription in commemoration of the marriage of Their Royal Highnesses, the Duke and Duchess of York on July 6th.1893." Further along we come to this rather splendid monument to William Poulsom whose story is very interesting.

Fig.173- Drinking Fountain, Derby Park

Wm.Poulsom

William Poulsom and his wife were big names in Bootle by 1880, the year that he was elected Mayor of the borough, even though he was not, at the time, an elected councillor.

His family were well-loved, partly due to Mrs.Poulsom's series of Winter Seasons of Cocoa-room Concerts, organised to help in the fight against the evils of drink. Both she and William were dedicated members of the Temperance movement, loathing the effect that alcohol had on the ordinary people.

Those attending the concerts were, at first, given a chit as they entered, this being exchanged for a cup of cocoa inside. Unfortunately, children hanging around outside collected the unused chits, so an admission charge of one penny was charged instead,

Fig.174- Poulsom Monument, Derby Park

all the cash being donated to charity.

Nights at these concerts must have been heady occasions for the times; performances included recitations, a ventriloquist, William Poulsom Jr. singing "The City Toff" and even the British Workman Cocoa-room Choir accompanied by Mrs.Poulsom on the piano! The grand venue for these occasions was the Lincoln Rooms on Derby Road.

Following his election as Mayor on 9th.Nov.1880, Poulsom's first official function was attendance at various church services on Hospital Sunday, traditionally the first Sabbath following the election of a new mayor. At the services, held in different churches in Bootle, sermons were preached to large congregations, whose generous contributions were used to help the hospital.

Even as soon as January 1881, it was being said that Poulsom would go down in history as Bootle's most popular mayor, partly due to his wife's enjoyable concerts, but his Temperance views also had considerable support. Later in the year, all households were questioned for their views on whether they were for or against Sunday opening of pubs. As the majority opposed such opening, Bootle made history by being the first area in England to go dry on Sundays!

Although, even now, Bootle preserves a haughty independence from its big brother Liverpool next door, it seems strange that, until Thursday 6th.Jan.1881, there was a toll bar across Stanley Road at the Bootle/Kirkdale boundary and for the previous 16 years it had cost travellers 6d. to enter Bootle and 3d. to leave it! So many detoured to avoid this bottleneck that it was abolished and Stanley Road adopted by Bootle Corporation. Unfortunately, adoption mean that they would have to repair the road as it had become very neglected. By a stroke of luck, the Tramways Company, eager

Fig.175- William Poulsom

Mrs.Poulsom

to get their tracks along this route, agreed to shoulder the major part of the cost of improving the road as they laid their lines down the middle.

It's fascinating to imagine the Bootle in which Poulsom lived. All those churches dotted around the central area were heavily used and wielded great influence in Society. It was in April 1881 that the Council discussed complaints by these churches of the nuisance caused by the Sarsfield Band and the Salvation Army Band as they paraded around the streets playing secular tunes on a Sunday, probably much to the enjoyment of most folk, but much to the annoyance of the worshippers who could hear them from inside!

Apparently, on one occasion, a crowd of "low people from the north end of Liverpool were extending all across the street" causing a little chaos! I'm sure that the "sally Army" weren't too perturbed by the complaints, but they didn't have it easy all the time. On one occasion that year they were marching down Kirkdale Road and Scotland Road singing hymns when they were attacked by a mob of 2,000 ruffians throwing stones, quite a frightening occasion!

On 28th.April 1881, Mr. Poulsom opened the 45th.Branch of the British Workman Public House Co. Ltd. at 48,Great Howard Street, this area being heavily poplulated at the time. Not a public house as we know it, but a cocoa-room in an area where it was estimated that no less than 100,000 men rose each morning, leaving home to go to work without a breakfast only to be confronted with an array of grog-shops ready to soak up his money and destroy his soul. At least he now had a choice of refreshment but, even though the cocoa-room opened at 4 am, what if all 100,000 arrived at once?

Many a mayor serves his term of office, giving of his services to his fellow men, his year of duties not involving any big occasion. Poulsom was one of the really lucky ones in that he was able to be involved in two really big events, the welcoming of Royalty and the opening of the new Town Hall!

The visit of the Prince & Princess of Wales was being arranged whereby they would arrive at Edge Hill, spend some time in Liverpool then sail into the newly-built North Docks, proceeding immediately back into Liverpool via Regent Road.

Even though they were technically Liverpool's docks, they were in Bootle and the residents of the Borough felt rather snubbed, to say the least, when they realised that they were to be ignored by the Royal visitors.

Poulsom took up the complaint and told Alderman A.B.Forwood of Liverpool that the itinery must be altered so that the Bootilians could see the Royalty and express their loyalty and love for them.

And so it was that, on Thursday 7th.Sept.1881, the Royal Couple arrived at Edge Hill, performed their functions in Liverpool, then sailed into the North Docks on the steamer Claughton to name one of the docks after the Princess, Alexandra.

The dock shed had been lavishly decorated for the enjoyment of the 1600 guests who sat down to a banquet, the Mayors of Liverpool and Bootle placed next to the Royal visitors. The procession left to travel over the Coffee House Bridge, Merton Road and Stanley Road.

The loyal population had decorated the streets in a manner second to none, even including London. The expected rain went away, the umbrellas coming in handy as shields against the scorching sunshine! Mr. & Mrs.Poulsom were loudly cheered by the spectators who knew that it was thanks to them that they had this spectacle to enjoy and, by arranging it, had, in effect, "put Bootle on the map" also helping it to assert its independence from Liverpool. At the boundary, Mr.Poulsom handed over his eminent guests into the care of the Mayor of Liverpool, his good deeds for the borough well done.

We cannot imagine what life was like in those days, when we consider that, at that time, electric light was only in an experimental form in the area around Liverpool Town Hall!

At a Council meeting on 9th.Nov.1881, it was enthusiastically decided that Mr.Poulsom should be re-elected as Mayor for a second year as recognition for his services to Bootle.

His second great day came when he opened the new Town Hall, designed by a Mr.Johnson in

Francis I Renaissance Style. The opening was carried out on Monday 10th April 1882, followed by a banquet. On Tuesday was held a Ball, Wednesday and Thursday it was open to the public to see where their money had been spent, and on Saturday was held a concert in aid of the Hospital. Also on this Saturday, it was Mrs.Poulsom's turn to be honoured by the presentation of an illuminated address in a casket. She was also presented with a solid silver dinner service, described even then as being costly, but paid for by subscriptions from ordinary people of the Borough. The presentation was made by Messrs. Tickle and Parkinson.

The Mayor was also at home to certain visitors during the week as well as all the other festivities. At their first Council meeting in the new building the following week, Poulsom's hospitality was praised, and at a Council meeting on Wed.14th.June he was presented with an illuminated address as a memento of his opening of the Town Hall. It was illustrated by artist James Orr Maples, placed in a red Morocco case which was decorated with gilt relief, the Bootle coat-of-arms and a portrait of Poulsom. The gold key with which he had opened the building had been suitably engraved for him as well. More will be aid of these buildings in Volume 2 of this book.

At the end of his two years in office, Poulsom was publicly praised for his labours on behalf of Bootle, some of which were done in his own time, purely for the pleasure of helping his fellow man, ably assisted by his incomparable wife who must have been a great source of inspiration and strength. He was also commended on his relentless fight for Temperance and for his impartiality in all affairs of both politics and religion.

Fig.178- Bootle Town Hall & Art Gallery

He was born in 1829 and just saw the New Century, dying in 1903, his life almost exactly matching the years of the reign of Queen Victoria. He was a man loved by all, and Bootle should have counted itself lucky to have had the services of such a man and his wife, not just in his term of office, but for many more years, working away out of the limelight, doing good for the folk that they loved.

Poulsom must have made a lasting impression on the Bootilians, because even though it was 13 years after his Mayoralty that Derby Park was opened, he and his wife were still fondly remembered by the locals who wanted "to commemorate the personal worth and public virtues of William Poulsom and Mary, his wife. This Memorial is erected by their fellow citizens."

Poulsom died in 1903, aged 74, having been Councillor, Alderman, Mayor and Chairman of Bootle Borough Hospitals. Part of the inscription on the memorial probably sums up his feelings on his life's works "Write me as one who loves his fellow men."

Stanley Gardens

On 6th.June 1902, to commemorate the coronation of Edward VII, Lord Derby donated to Bootle the North and South Recreation Grounds on a 999-year lease and made a gift of what is now known as Stanley Gardens.

It was on 18th.July 1904 that the gardens were opened by Lord Derby, the Countess unveiling the statue of Edward VII which had been presented to Bootle by Colonel Sandys, MP for the Borough.

The War Memorial, of quite exceptional design and quality, was presented by the Memorial Committee which had been formed after the Great War, and was unveiled by Major James Burnie M.C. on 15th.Oct.1922. It was designed by H.Cawthra R.B.S. and bears the inscription "In Grateful Memory of over 1,000 men from Bootle

Fig.177- Poulsom Monument, top figure

who made the Supreme Sacrifice in the Great War 1914-18 and 1939-45."

Take a good look at the figures of the Airman, Soldier and Marine, they are of exceptional quality and would look well in any city in the land. The top figure of mother and child probably signifies Peace and the future for which they were fighting.

Fig.179- King Edward VII statue, Stanley Gardens

Fig.181- War Memorial, The Sailor/Marine

Fig.180- War Memorial, The Soldier

Fig.182- War Memorial, The Airman

Fig.183- War Memorial, top figure of Christian Charity

Drinking Fountains

The father of drinking fountains in this country was Charles Pierre Melly, born in Tue Brook on 25th.May 1829. His father was André Melly of Geneva and his mother Ellen Greg of Quarry Bank, Wilmslow. The family were involved in cotton mills and were the first ones to import cotton from Egypt. Quarry Bank Mill is now open to the public and is well worth a visit to learn of the Gregs and their industry.

The trade with Egypt prospered, Charles Melly spending quite a time there seeing the sights. Tourism completed, he returned home to join the family firm of Melly, Forget & Co., which by now were involved in the American trade. Melly spent quite a lot of time at the waterfront, supervising the business and couldn't help noticing that there was nowhere for the ordinary working man to quench his thirst without spending his meagre wages in a pub., when he didn't really want ale, but just a drink of water.

In his father's home of Geneva, it was a common sight to see drinking fountains in the street, and Melly decided that he would try to get some introduced here. He did a deal with the Corporation whereby he provided the fountains if they supplied the water. His fountains were simple, in red granite, and he went to great pains to impress upon the owners of the walls that very few bricks would have to be removed to accommodate them.

Fig.184- Drinking fountain, Princes Dock, 1854

Because of this simplicity of design, they are easily overlooked. His first fountains were installed in 1854 and a list of them survives in the Picton Library. The one shown is an 1854 one at Princes Dock, one of the very first drinking fountains in Britain! As far as I know, only one still retains its lion-head spout, a fountain in the South end of Liverpool. Other Melly fountains can be found dotted all over the older parts of the City, including one in the graveyard wall of Walton Church, dated 1861, one outside St.Anne's Church, Prescot Road, outside St.Michael's Church, West Derby Road near Ogdens and one opposite the Steble Fountain in William Brown St.

The fountains originally were provided with a continuous flow of water as it was found that taps soon wore out due to heavy usage. Melly is reputed to have spent £500 on this project, a lot of money in those days, but he pressed ahead and attempted to have them introduced in other towns as well.

I even discovered one on Platform 5 of Crewe Station, dated 1863, with the addition of a little ground level pool bearing a cast-iron label "For Ye Dogs!" Look out for it next time you go to London, it is nicely restored and instantly recognisable as a Melly fountain!

His work was praised in the "Daily News" of 1st.July 1858, commenting that there was not a single drinking fountain anywhere in London! Soon after this,there was formed the Metropolitan Drinking Fountain and Cattle Trough Association, which got things moving in the Capital! Their creations are quite magnificent and can be seen in various places including a site near Bank Station.

It will be noticed that all other fountains in Liverpool and, indeed other places as well, date after 1854 so it looks like the idea spread, encouraging other donors to follow his lead. The ironic thing is that, in 1990, there is still nowhere to go for a drink of water, so we are obliged to enter a pub. or cafe in search of refreshment! Never a man to be idle, Melly went on to provide wayside seats for weary travellers and swings for children, making playgrounds on spare land which would be loaned to him until it was eventually built upon as the city expanded. On 31st.May 1858 he opened a Gymnasium and Playground at the corner of Chatsworth Street for the benefit of the Working Classes.

A collection was started through the Daily Post by folk writing in and signing themselves "A working man" and, on Nov. 6th. 1861, he was presented with a silver candelabrum, costing over 200 Gns., engraved with messages of recognition for his gifts of fountains, seats and playgrounds.

Melly later served in the army in the Childwall Rifles and then became involved in the planning of Sefton Park, becoming Chairman of the Sefton Park Committee and of the Water Committee. It was he who persuaded them to employ M.André of Paris to design the grottoes, hoping that when Lake Vyrnwy was built, enough water would be available to cascade through them.

The Park was commenced in 1867, the turning of the first sod being the scene of a great mock battle between the Duke of Cambridge and the Liverpool Volunteers! The park was opened by Prince Arthur on Whit Monday 1872.

It was on 9th.Nov.1888 that Charles Pierre Melly took a last walk in the Sefton Park that he loved; the following day he died, having lived a long and happy life. Happy eccentricity seems to run in the Melly family, because it was the intrepid Henry Melly who flew his own plane around the Mersey as early as 30th.May 1911!

Happily, the Melly family still reside on Merseyside and are related to our own George Melly, the gifted and outrageously funny entertainer and jazz singer, who told me that his ancestor, Charles Pierre, used to lie in bed, delighting at the thought of all the little trickles of water running all over Liverpool!

Fig.185- A Melly Fountain water spout

Boundary Posts and Markers

The City and, indeed, the Country as a whole, is littered with markers and posts of all ages indicating the boundaries of districts and areas, some now part of history , but all of interest as part of the street scene.

Probably the oldest, and certainly the most interesting that I have found, is outside the Abbey pub. at the corner of Walton Lane and Tetlow Street. The inscription reads "Borough of Liverpool 1865, Erected by the Health Committee. Town Hall 2 miles 825 yards. Height above Old Dock sill 145.5 feet". There's all the information that you need should you have lost your bearings as you stagger out of the pub. in a delicate state!

Not too far away at the corner of Priory Road Anfield and Townsend Lane, stands a really gorgeous marker "Erected by the Overseers 1884" and marking the boundary of the "Township of Walton on the Hill" and "Township of West Derby". Similar posts can be found in Cherry Lane, near Richard Kelly Drive, Seeds Lane near Melling Road and Moss Lane, Orrell Park. The inscriptions on the first two are too indistinct to be legible but the latter one is dated 1887 and marks the Walton-on-the-Hill/Bootle boundary.

At the corner of Breck Road and Lower Breck Road is a little stone marker which carries some obscure inscription and the date, possibly 1817.

While on the subject of West Derby, note should be made of a cast iron marker, at the corner

Fig.186- Boundary post, Walton Lane/Tetlow Street

of West Derby Road and Belmont Road, which states "West Derby Local Board District Boundary 1868."

The Township of West Derby was once extremely large, but nearby Liverpool was expanding at an alarming rate as industrialisation boomed. In 1835 Liverpool Municipal Borough took over part of West Derby, leaving 2,594 acres outside the Liverpool boundary.

This was governed by a Local Board which became an Urban District, in 1894, being dissolved the following year as Liverpool expanded still further.

It was this local board which was responsible for the building of Fazakerley Sewage Farm, still in use today.

In the Mossley Hill area are a few items of interest, the older areas being happy hunting grounds for seekers of history and its relics. At the Aigburth Road/Ashfield Road corner, a lovely iron plate tells us that it is 3½ miles to Liverpool Exchange. This was at the beginning of a turnpike road, designed to lure the rich merchants and others out to the newly developed area of Toxteth. As is the case today, communication is a most important factor in the selling of a site.

It is possible that the very small stone marker, bearing the letters TTP, at the corner of North Mossley Hill Road and Ibbotson's Lane, could be

Fig.187- Boundary Post, Townsend Lane/Priory Road Anfield

Fig. 188- Boundary Post, Townsend Lane/Priory Road Anfield

Fig. 189- Boundary post, Breck Road/Lower Breck Road

Fig. 190- Boundary Post, Belmont Road

Fig. 191- Boundary Post, Aigburth Road

Fig. 192- Boundary Post, North Mossley Hill Road

marking part of the route of the Toxteth Turnpike.

Outside Mossley Hill Church in Elmswood Road, a small stone marker shows the Wavertree/Garston boundary and outside 26, Rose Lane is one for the Allerton/Wavertree border.

Fig.193- Boundary Post, outside Mossley Hill Church

The railway companies also marked the limits of their land, and where the main London line crosses Smithdown Road, there are to be seen about three semi circular markers in the pavement, boundaries of the London & North Western Railway Co..

The former Lancashire & Yorkshire Railway, which still runs as Merseyrail through Walton, once had the stone marker shown. This was at the edge of their land at the top of Mosedale Road, off Rice Lane but, sadly, was thrown away with the builder's rubble on construction of a new fence to keep out vandals. What a shame that it was discarded after standing there for 100 years.

Fig.195- Boundary plate, Smithdown Road

Fig.194- Boundary post, outside 26, Rose Lane

Fig.196- Boundary Post, Mosedale Road

Cemeteries

Given the time, cemeteries can be an endless source of interesting information and are a study in themselves. An example is the obelisk situated near the entrance doors to the Anglican Cathedral. An unusual feature is a carved head which is let into a niche near the base of the monument.

The inscription reads: "This monument was erected by the Gandy Belt Manufacturing Co.Ltd. in Grateful Memory of its Founder, Maurice Gandy, who died 22/12/1892".

Mr.Gandy lived at The Cliff, Wellington Road, New Brighton and, when he died, left only £28.35 to his widow, Elizabeth. It doesn't seem a lot for a managing director to leave in his will, does it?

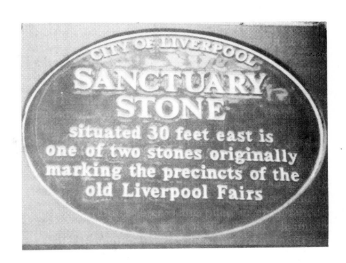

Fig.198- Sanctuary Stone, plaque in Castle Street

Fig.197- Liverpool Cathedral, The Gandy Obelisk

Sanctuary Stone

Set into the road surface of Castle Street, on the side nearest the river, is a round stone known as the Sanctuary Stone. The area between this and another such stone in Dale Street (now gone) offered sanctuary for debtors at certain times, provided they were of good behavior.

For ten days before and ten days after the two fairs that, until an Act of 1696, were held on 25th.July and 11th.Nov. of each year, the debtors could escape arrest.

Appendix

Hillsborough Memorial

Happily, the age of monument-building is not over as can be seen from this quite magnificent and tasteful Sudley Sundial created by sculptor David Strachan of Messrs. Evans & Burkey of Smithdown Road.

The inscription says that "This Sundial was erected by the people of Aigburth and Mossley Hill and paid for by public subscription in memory of the 95 Liverpool FC supporters who died at Hillsborough on 15th.April 1989"

It was on that day that so many people were crushed, some fatally, against the iron railings at the edge of that football pitch. Feelings understandably ran high, tributes later being piled in abundance at the Ground here in Liverpool. The inevitable inquiry was held, blaming the Police for their inefficient handling of the crowds, while they, in turn, blamed the fans.

For those of us who weren't there, we can only try to imagine the horror of it all but, at least, in this quiet and peaceful garden at the rear of the Sudley Art Gallery, the souls of those departed can be remembered for all time. Commemorated are 20 year-old Stephen Copoc, groundsman at Sudley Gardens, 19 year-old student Sarah Hicks who was resident at nearby Carnatic Halls and her 15 year-old sister, Victoria. Also remembered is Peter McDonnell, 21.

The memorial was unveiled on Sunday, 29th.October 1989 by the Rev.Kenneth Lane, Aigburth Methodist Minister. His Boy's Brigade Company, of which one of the dead boys, 14 year-old Phillip Hammond, had been a member, formed the guard of honour. His brother, Graham, laid a wreath of flowers at the base.

Sufficient money was raised to provide two teak seats from which visitors can ponder the loss of their friends. One is inscribed "Rest A while and Remember" while the other, on the patio at the rear of the Art Gallery, was made by the Aigburth Opportunities YTS workers and is a truly beautiful piece of work.

Summing it all up, the carved rose on the front of the plinth is framed by the words "Time marches on; we will always remember".

Bootle

This marvellous monument has suddenly sprung up in a small garden in Southport Road, Bootle, near the junction of Breeze Hill. It formerly stood at the top of Merton Road and was removed in the late fifties to make way for the Mark Connolly Island (see page 66). In May 1989, it was taken out of storage, cleaned and re-erected on this site, complete with its light, proudly shining high above the surrounding area.

It was originally dedicated to Edward Geoffrey Stanley, 14th. Earl of Derby and was erected by a few of the inhabitants of Bootle as a memorial of their respect and esteem. Strangely, there is no date on the structure.

Fig.199- Hillsborough Memorial

Fig.200- Southport Road, Bootle

Index

Part Two

Part Two of "Well, I Never Noticed That!"

The second part will examine, in detail, the decoration of Liverpool and Bootle's buildings and its meaning. Sometimes such embellishments were mere stock items chosen from a builder's catalogue, but mostly they represent the use of the building or the occupation of its owners. Liverpool has some of the most lavishly ornamented buildings outside London and the research into this subject has been both fascinating and intensive.

Readers interested in acquiring Part Two should write to West Derby Publishing who will inform them of publication date.

Acknowledgements

As both parts of this book were originally conceived as one volume, it has been decided to publish a complete list of acknowledgements and bibliography in Part Two.

The Author

The Author is resident in Liverpool and is already known for his Guide Book to St.George's Hall. It is hoped that other such guide books will follow in due course.

Also by the same author:

"Civic Pride No.1" the official guidebook to Liverpool's St.George's Hall. Fifteen pages, lavishly illustrated and available at Liverpool bookshops or from the publishers at £2.00 incl.

Published by West Derby Publishing,
279, Eaton Road, Liverpool Ll2 2AG.
Text and all illustrations are copyright of the publisher, unauthorised reproduction prohibited.
ISBN 1 871075 02 5

British Library Cataloguing in Publication Data
Richardson, Andrew F.
The Statues & Monuments of Liverpool and Bootle,
– (Well, I Never Noticed That!; Pt. 1)
1. Merseyside (Metropolitan County), Liverpool –
visitor's guides.
I. Title II, Series
914.275304858
ISBN 1-871075-02-5.